SEC. 125 CR. P. C.- SUPREME COURT'S LEADING CASE LAWS

CASE NOTES- FACTS- FINDINGS OF APEX COURT JUDGES & CITATIONS

JAYPRAKASH BANSILAL SOMANI

Dedicated

To

All the Past & Present Judges of the Supreme Court of India.

Salute to their wisdom.

Salute to their interpretation of Law.

Salute to their elaborative judgement writing.

Contents

Preface

Dear Learned Advocates of the Trial Courts, Family Court, Session Courts, Tribunals, High Courts, Supreme Court & Individuals,

I am very delighted to provide you a book on 'SEC. 125 CR. P. C.- Supreme Court of India's Leading Case Laws'.

In this book you will get...

1. Name of the Case i. e. Cause title

2.Relevant Sections discussed in the case

3. Hon'ble Judges/Coram of the case

4.Number of PDF Pages in Original Judgement of the case

5. All available Citations of the case

6. Case Note with appeal allowed/ dismissed or disposed off

7. Facts of the case

8. Hon'ble Apex Court's findings, while dismissing/allowing or disposing the appeal

9. Ratio Decidendi if any.

My special thanks to Manupatra, because of their web portal I can compile this book in well manner. I am also thankful to Notion Press to support me to publish & market this book throughout the Country. Thanks to my Juniors, Advocate Colleagues & Insolvency Professional Colleagues to support me in this venture.

Adv. Aqsa Sahar has helped me a lot to compile this book.

I hope this book will add some value addition in the wealth of your legal knowledge. Your positive feedbacks will boost me to compile/ write further books & negative feedbacks will improve my skills. Kindly send your valuable feedbacks by email.

Thanks with Regards,

Jayprakash B. Somani

Advocate, Supreme Court of India

Email: jaysomani64@gmail.com

Web Site:www.jayprakashsomani.com

Call: 9318381287, 8384051134, 9322188701.

Acknowledgements

Printed & Published by
Notion Press
No. 8, 3rd Cross Street,
CIT Colony, Mylapore,
Chennai, Tamil Nadu- 600004

Managed by
Jayprakash Somani Advocates & Solicitors
Law Firm for Supreme Court of India
Delhi Office
257 C, Pocket 1, Mayur Vihar Phase 1, Delhi 110091.
Call 9318381287, 8384051134, 9322188701, 8459194576.
Supreme Court Chamber
312, 3rd Floor, M. C. Setalvad Block, In front of 'D' Gate, Bhagwan Das Road, Supreme Court of India, New Delhi 110001
Contact: 8459194576, 9811011747,
www.jayprakashsomani.com

Books are available online at
1. Notion Press: https://notionpress.com/author/jayprakash_somani
2. Amazon: https://www.amazon.in/s?k=jayprakash+somani
3. Flipkart: https://www.flipkart.com/search?q=Jayprakash%20Somani

CHAPTER ONE

Sanjeev Kapoor Vs. Chandana Kapoor and Ors., 2020

Hon'ble Judges/Coram:

Ashok Bhushan and R. Subhash Reddy, JJ.

Relevant Section:

Code of Criminal Procedure, 1973 (CrPC) - Section 125; Code of Criminal Procedure, 1973 (CrPC) - Section 362

No. of pdf pages of Original Judgment : 11

Equivalent citations:

AIR2020SC1064, 2020 (1) ALD(Crl.) 730 (SC), 2020(2)BLJ324, 2020(3)Crimes474(SC), 2020(2)CTC740, I(2020)DMC696SC, 2020(2)HLR1, 2020(2)J.L.J.R.19, 2020(2)JKJ289[SC], 2020(3)JLJ117, 2020 (2) KHC 345, 2020(2)KLT267, 2020-2-LW(Crl)838, 2020(I)OLR745, 2020(2)PLJR19, 2020(2)RCR(Criminal)105, 2021(3)RLW1701(SC), (2020)13SCC172, 2020 (6) SCJ 390, 2020(1)UC634 MANU/SC/0209/2020

Case Note:

Family - Maintenance - Review of order - Sections 125, 125(1), 125(3), 125(5) and 362 of Code of Criminal Procedure, 1973 - Appellant was married to Respondent and daughter and son was born out of their wedlock - Application under Section 125 of Code was filed by Respondent No. 1 against her husband claiming maintenance - Appellant filed petition for divorce against Respondent No. 1 - On reconciliation efforts made by Family Court parties settled matter amicably on terms and conditions - Maintenance petition was, thus, disposed of by Family Court - Respondent

No. 1 filed application under Section 125(3) of Code for enforcement of maintenance order being Execution Petition which stand rejected by Family Court - Thereafter, Respondent No. 1 filed application for recalling of order passed in maintenance petition and for restoring application filed under Section 125(3) of Code - Additional Principal Judge, Family Court set aside order passed in maintenance petition and restoring petition under Section 125 of Code - Appellant filed application in High Court against order passed by Family Court which stand rejected - Hence, present appeal - Whether embargo contained in under Section 362 of Code prohibiting court to alter or review its judgment or final order disposing case applies to order passed under Section 125 of Code.

Facts:

The Appellant was married to Respondent No. 1and a daughter and son was born out of their wedlock. An application under Section 125 Code of Criminal Procedure was filed by Respondent No. 1 against her husband claiming maintenance for Respondent No. 1 as well as Respondent Nos. 2 and 3, minor daughter and son. The Appellant filed a petition for divorce against Respondent No. 1. On the reconciliation efforts made by the Family Court parties settled the matter amicably on the terms and conditions recorded separately in the Court. As per the settlement the Appellant was to pay amount towards the maintenance of the Respondents. The maintenance petition was, thus, disposed of by the Family Court. Respondent No. 1 filed an application under Section 125(3) Code of Criminal Procedure for enforcement of the order being Execution Petition. The Execution Petition filed by Respondent No. 1 was rejected by the Additional Principal Judge, Family Court. The Court held that order being purely conditional and was subject to the fulfilment of the respective obligations by the parties which they have not performed, the application under Section 125(3) Code of Criminal Procedure was not maintainable. After the application filed by Respondent No. 1 for execution of the order was rejected, Respondent No. 1 filed an application for recall the order passed in maintenance petition. Respondent No. 1 prayed that order be recalled and application under Section 125(3) of Code be restored and decided on merits after hearing the parties. The Additional Principal Judge, Family Court set aside the order restoring the petition under Section 125 Code of Criminal Procedure Challenging the order passed by the Family Court, the Appellant had filed application in the High Court which had been rejected by the High Court.

Hon'ble Apex Court held, while dismissing/allowing the appeals:

Held, while dismissing the appeal:

(i) The Legislative Scheme indicates that Magistrate did not become functus officio after passing an order under Section 125 Code of Criminal Procedure, as and when occasion arises the Magistrate exercises the jurisdiction from time to time. By Section 125(5) Code of Criminal Procedure, Magistrate is expressly empowered to cancel an order passed under Section 125(1) Code of Criminal Procedure on fulfilment of certain conditions.

(ii) Section 127 Code of Criminal Procedure also discloses the legislative intendment where the Magistrate is empowered to alter an order passed under Section 125 Code of Criminal Procedure Sub-section (2) of Section 127 Code of Criminal Procedure also empower the Magistrate to cancel or vary an order under Section 125. The Legislative Scheme as delineated by Sections 125 and 127 Code of Criminal Procedure clearly enumerated the circumstances and incidents provided in the Code of Criminal Procedure where Court passing a judgment or final order disposing the case can alter or review the same. The embargo as contained in Section 362 was, thus, clearly relaxed in proceeding under Section 125 Code of Criminal Procedure.

(iii) It had come on the record that after passing of the order on settlement, the Appellant according to his own case has paid only an amount of One Lakh Rupees, i.e. maintenance of four months. The arrears had not been paid by the Appellant within six months which was time allowed by the Court. When the Appellant did not honour its commitment under settlement, could the wife be left in lurch by not able to press for grant of maintenance on non-compliance by the Appellant of the terms of settlement. The answer was obviously No. Section 125 Code of Criminal Procedure had to be interpreted in a manner as to advance justice and to protect a woman for whose benefit the provisions had been engrafted.

(iv)The order passed in present case by Family Court reviving the maintenance application of the wife under Section 125 Code of Criminal Procedure by setting aside order passed on settlement was not hit by the embargo contained in Section 362 Code of Criminal Procedure. The submission of the Appellant that Section 362 Code of Criminal Procedure prohibit the Magistrate to pass the impugned order could not be accepted.

Disposition:

Appeal Dismissed

CHAPTER TWO

AJAY KUMAR VS. LATA AND ORS., 2019

Hon'ble Judges/Coram:

Dr. D.Y. Chandrachud and Hemant Gupta, JJ.

Relevant Section:

CRIMINAL MATTERS - MATTERS RELATING TO HARASSMENT, CRUELTY TO WOMAN FOR DOWRY, DOWRY DEATH, EVE-TEASING, DOMESTIC VIOLENCE ETC.

No. of pdf pages of Original Judgment: 5

Equivalent citations:

2021(1)ACR254, 2019(202)AIC101, AIR2019SC2600, 2020 (1) ALD(Crl.) 218 (SC), 2019 (109) ACC 217, 2019(4)BLJ73, 2019 (2) CCC 452 , 2019(3)CGLJ220, 2019CriLJ3344, 2019(2)Crimes359(SC), 260(2019)DLT35, II(2019)DMC241SC, 2019(2)HLR411, 2019(3)JCC1946, 2019(2)JKJ123[SC], 2019(2)JLJ595, 2019 (3) KHC 164, 2019(2)KLJ963, 2019(II)OLR167, 2019(2)RCR(Criminal)1016, 2019(2)RLW1671(SC), 2019(7)SCALE193, (2019)15SCC352 MANU/SC/0651/2019

Case Note:

Family - Payment of maintenance - Issuance of direction - Sections 12, 20 2(q) and 2(s) of Protection of Women from Domestic Violence Act, 2005 - Present appeal arose from a judgment of a learned Single Judge of High Court dismissing a petition against judgment of Additional Sessions Judge, confirming an interim order for award of maintenance to first Respondent and her minor child under the provisions of Act, 2005 - Whether impugned directions for payment of maintenance were liable to be set aside.

Facts:

The first Respondent was married to Vijay Kumar Jindal on 12 December 2019. They have two children. The first Respondent filed a petition under Section 12 of the Act for the purpose of seeking an award of maintenance. The complaint contains a recital of the fact that after her marriage, the complainant and her spouse resided at a house which constitutes ancestral Hindu Joint Family Property. She and her husband resided on the ground floor of the residential accommodation. The Appellant and the deceased spouse of the first Respondent jointly carried on a business of a kiryana store at Panipat from which, it has been alleged, each had an income of about Rs. 30,000 per month. The complaint alleges that, at the death of Vijay Kumar, the first Respondent was pregnant and that she gave birth to a child on 31 January 2013. The travails of the first Respondent are alleged to have commenced after the death of her spouse and she was not permitted to reside in her matrimonial home. The learned Trial Judge by an order granted monthly maintenance in the amount of Rs. 4,000 to the first Respondent and Rs. 2,000 to the second Respondent. The award of maintenance was directed against the Appellant who was carrying on the above business together with the deceased spouse of the first Respondent. This order of the Judicial Magistrate, was confirmed by the Additional Sessions Judge. The High Court, in a petition filed by the Appellant, affirmed the view. Hence, present proceedings.

Hon'ble Apex Court held, while dismissing/allowing the appeals:

Held, while disposing of the appeal

1. The submission which has been urged on behalf of the Appellant is that there was no basis under the provisions of the Act to fasten liability on the Appellant, who is the brother of the deceased spouse of the first Respondent. Learned Counsel submitted that the sole basis on which liability has been fastened is that the Appellant and his deceased brother carried on a joint business. This cannot furnish any lawful basis to direct the Appellant to meet the award of maintenance.

2. Section 12(1) provides that an aggrieved person may present an application to the Magistrate seeking one or more reliefs under the Act. Under the provisions of Section 20(1), the Magistrate while dealing with an application Under Sub-section (1) of Section 12 is empowered to direct the Respondent(s) to pay monetary relief to meet the expenses incurred and losses suffered by the aggrieved person and any child of the aggrieved person as a result of domestic violence. This may include but is not limited to an order for maintenance of the aggrieved person as well as her children,

if any, including an order under or in addition to an order for maintenance under Section 125 of CrPC or any other law for the time being in force.

3. The substantive part of Section 2(q) indicates that the expression "Respondent" means any adult male person who is, or has been, in a domestic relationship with the aggrieved person and against whom relief has been sought. The proviso indicates that both, an aggrieved wife or a female living in a relationship in the nature of marriage may also file a complaint against a relative of the husband or the male partner, as the case may be.

4. Section 2(f) defines the expression 'domestic relationship' to mean a relationship where two persons live or have lived together at any point of time in a shared household when they are related by consanguinity, marriage or through a relationship in the nature of marriage, adoption or are members living together as a joint family.

5. The expression "shared household" is defined in Section 2(s) as a household where the person aggrieved lives or at any stage has lived in a domestic relationship either singly or along with the Respondent and includes such a house hold whether owned or tenanted either jointly by the aggrieved person and the Respondent, or owned or tenanted by either of them in respect of which either the aggrieved person or the Respondent or both jointly or singly have any right, title, interest or equity and includes such a household which may belong to the joint family of which the Respondent is a member, irrespective of whether the Respondent or the aggrieved person has any right, title or interest in the shared household.

6. All these definitions indicate the width and amplitude of the intent of Parliament in creating both an obligation and a remedy in the terms of the enactment.

7. At the present stage, there are sufficient averments in the complaint to sustain the order for the award of interim maintenance. Paragraph 10 of the complaint prima facie indicates that, the case of the complainants is that the house where the first Respondent and her spouse resided, belong to a joint family. The Appellant and his brother (who was the spouse of the first Respondent and father of the second Respondent) carried on a joint business. The Appellant resided in the same household. Ultimately, whether the requirements of Section 2(f); Section 2(q); and Section 2(s) are fulfilled is a matter of evidence which will be adjudicated upon at the trial. At this stage, for the purpose of an interim order for maintenance, there was material which justifies the issuance of a direction in regard to the

payment of maintenance.

8. The Appeal is, accordingly, disposed of.

Ratio Decidendi: An aggrieved wife or a female living in a relationship in nature of marriage is entitled to maintenance, against a relative of the husband or the male partner

Disposition:

Disposed of

CHAPTER THREE

SWAPAN KUMAR BANERJEE VS. THE STATE OF WEST BENGAL AND ORS., 2019

Hon'ble Judges/Coram:

Deepak Gupta and Aniruddha Bose, JJ.

Relevant Section:

CRIMINAL MATTERS - MATTERS RELATING TO MAINTENANCE UNDER SECTION 125 OF CR.P.C.

No. of pdf pages of the Original Judgment : 5

Equivalent citations:

AIR2019SC4748, 2019 (2) ALD(Crl.) 1008 (SC), 2019 (3) ALT (Crl.) 326 (A.P.), 2021(4)BLJ181, 2020CriLJ330, 2019(4)Crimes170(SC), 2019(6)CTC340, III(2019)DMC594SC, 2019(3)HLR392, 2019(5)JKJ320[SC], 2019 (4) KHC 881, 2019(4)KLJ547, 2019(4)KLT63, 2019(4)RCR(Criminal)628 MANU/SC/1343/2019

Case Note:

Family - Maintenance - Desertion - Section 125 of Code of Criminal Procedure, 1973 - Husband filing petition of judicial separation, though, it was alleged that wife had deserted him - Petition for divorce was filed and divorce was granted - When wife was living separately from her husband she did not file any petition for grant of maintenance - Even during divorce proceedings though application under Section 24 of Act was filed but it seems that same was either dismissed for non-prosecution or was not pressed - Hence, present appeal - Whether wife, who had been divorced by husband, on ground that wife had deserted him, was entitled to claim maintenance under Section 125 of Code.

Facts:

The matrimonial dispute started with the husband filing a petition of judicial separation, though, it was alleged that the wife had deserted him. A petition for divorce was filed and the divorce was granted. When the wife was living separately from her husband she did not file any petition for grant of maintenance. Even during the divorce proceedings though an application under Section 24 of the Hindu Marriage Act, 1955 was filed but it seems that the same was either dismissed for non-prosecution or was not pressed.

Hon'ble Apex Court held, while dismissing/allowing the appeals:

Held, while dismissing the appeal:

(i) Once the relationship of marriage comes to an end, the woman obviously was not under any obligation to live with her former husband. The deeming fiction of the divorced wife being treated as a wife can only be read for the limited purpose for grant of maintenance and the deeming fiction cannot be stretched to the illogical extent that the divorced wife is under a compulsion to live with the ex-husband. The husband could not urge that he can divorce his wife on the ground that she had deserted him and then deny maintenance which should otherwise be payable to her on the ground that even after divorce she was not willing to live with him.

(ii) After the divorce was granted, according to the Appellant he got remarried after a year and it was only thereafter that the wife filed a petition for grant of maintenance. That, would make no difference because it was for the wife to decide when she wants to file a petition for maintenance. She may have felt comfortable with whatever earnings she had upto that time or may be she did not want to precipitate matters till she was contesting the divorce petition by filing a claim for maintenance. Whatever be the reason, the mere fact that the wife did not file a petition for grant of maintenance during the pendency of the matrimonial proceedings, was no ground to hold that she is not entitled to file such a petition later on.

(iii) The issue raised was that the wife being a qualified architect from a reputed university would be presumed to have sufficient income. It was pertinent to mention that as far as the husband was concerned, his income through taxable returns had been brought on record which shows that he was earning a substantial amount and on that basis amount had been awarded as monthly maintenance to the wife. No evidence had been led to show what was the income of the wife or where the wife was working. It was for the husband to lead such evidence. In the absence of any such evidence no presumption could be raised that the wife was earning sufficient amount to support herself.

Disposition:

Appeal Dismissed

Hon'ble Judges/Coram:

Deepak Gupta and Aniruddha Bose, JJ.

Relevant Section:

CRIMINAL MATTERS - MATTERS RELATING TO MAINTENANCE UNDER SECTION 125 OF CR.P.C.

No. of pdf pages of the Original Judgment : 5

Equivalent citations:

AIR2019SC4748, 2019 (2) ALD(Crl.) 1008 (SC), 2019 (3) ALT (Crl.) 326 (A.P.), 2021(4)BLJ181, 2020CriLJ330, 2019(4)Crimes170(SC), 2019(6)CTC340, III(2019)DMC594SC, 2019(3)HLR392, 2019(5)JKJ320[SC], 2019 (4) KHC 881, 2019(4)KLJ547, 2019(4)KLT63, 2019(4)RCR(Criminal)628 MANU/SC/1343/2019

Case Note:

Family - Maintenance - Desertion - Section 125 of Code of Criminal Procedure, 1973 - Husband filing petition of judicial separation, though, it was alleged that wife had deserted him - Petition for divorce was filed and divorce was granted - When wife was living separately from her husband she did not file any petition for grant of maintenance - Even during divorce proceedings though application under Section 24 of Act was filed but it seems that same was either dismissed for non-prosecution or was not pressed - Hence, present appeal - Whether wife, who had been divorced by husband, on ground that wife had deserted him, was entitled to claim maintenance under Section 125 of Code.

Facts:

The matrimonial dispute started with the husband filing a petition of judicial separation, though, it was alleged that the wife had deserted him. A petition for divorce was filed and the divorce was granted. When the wife was living separately from her husband she did not file any petition for grant of maintenance. Even during the divorce proceedings though an application under Section 24 of the Hindu Marriage Act, 1955 was filed but it seems that the same was either dismissed for non-prosecution or was not pressed.

Hon'ble Apex Court held, while dismissing/allowing the appeals:

Held, while dismissing the appeal:

(i) Once the relationship of marriage comes to an end, the woman obviously was not under any obligation to live with her former husband. The deeming fiction of the divorced wife being treated as a wife can only be read for the limited purpose for grant of maintenance and the deeming fiction cannot be stretched to the illogical extent that the divorced wife is under a compulsion to live with the ex-husband. The husband could not urge that he can divorce his wife on the ground that she had deserted him and then deny maintenance which should otherwise be payable to her on the ground that even after divorce she was not willing to live with him.

(ii) After the divorce was granted, according to the Appellant he got remarried after a year and it was only thereafter that the wife filed a petition for grant of maintenance. That, would make no difference because it was for the wife to decide when she wants to file a petition for maintenance. She may have felt comfortable with whatever earnings she had upto that time or may be she did not want to precipitate matters till she was contesting the divorce petition by filing a claim for maintenance. Whatever be the reason, the mere fact that the wife did not file a petition for grant of maintenance during the pendency of the matrimonial proceedings, was no ground to hold that she is not entitled to file such a petition later on.

(iii) The issue raised was that the wife being a qualified architect from a reputed university would be presumed to have sufficient income. It was pertinent to mention that as far as the husband was concerned, his income through taxable returns had been brought on record which shows that he was earning a substantial amount and on that basis amount had been awarded as monthly maintenance to the wife. No evidence had been led to show what was the income of the wife or where the wife was working. It was for the husband to lead such evidence. In the absence of any such evidence no presumption could be raised that the wife was earning sufficient amount to support herself.

Disposition:

Appeal Dismissed

CHAPTER FOUR

RAJNESH VS. NEHA AND ORS., 2020

Hon'ble Judges/Coram:

Indu Malhotra and R. Subhash Reddy, JJ.

Relevant Section:

HINDU MARRAIGE ACT, 1955 - SECTION 28A; CODE OF CRIMINAL PROCEDURE, 1973 (CrPC) - SECTION 128; PROTECTION OF WOMEN FROM DOMESTIC VOILENCE ACT, 2005 - Section 20 MATTERS RELATING TO MAINTENANCE UNDER SECTION 125 OF CR.P.C.

No. of pdf pages of Original judgment: 5

Equivalent citations:

AIR2019SC4748, 2019 (2) ALD(Crl.) 1008 (SC), 2019 (3) ALT (Crl.) 326 (A.P.), 2021(4)BLJ181, 2020CriLJ330, 2019(4)Crimes170(SC), 2019(6)CTC340, III(2019)DMC594SC, 2019(3)HLR392, 2019(5)JKJ320[SC], 2019 (4) KHC 881, 2019(4)KLJ547, 2019(4)KLT63, 2019(4)RCR(Criminal)628 MANU/SC/0833/2020

Case Note:

Family - Maintenance - Guidelines thereto - Respondent No. 1-wife left matrimonial home shortly after birth of son-Respondent No. 2 - Wife filed application for interim maintenance under Section 125 of Code on behalf of herself and minor son - Family Court awarded interim maintenance to Respondent No. 1-wife and Respondent No. 2-son - Appellant-husband challenged Order of Family Court filed before High Court - High Court dismissed Writ Petition and affirmed Judgment passed by Family Court - Hence, present appeal - Whether there was need to frame guidelines on certain aspects pertaining to payment of maintenance in matrimonial matters.

Facts:

The Respondent No. 1-wife left matrimonial home shortly after the birth of the son-Respondent No. 2. The wife filed an application for interim maintenance under Section 125 Code of Criminal Procedure on behalf of herself and the minor son. The Family Court vide a detailed Order awarded interim maintenance to the Respondent No. 1-wife and Respondent No. 2-son. The Appellant-husband challenged the Order of the Family Court vide Criminal Writ Petition filed before the High Court, Nagpur Bench. The High Court dismissed the Writ Petition and affirmed the Judgment passed by the Family Court. This Court issued notice to the wife and directed the Appellant-husband to file his Income Tax Returns and Assessment Orders. He was also directed to place a photocopy of his passport on record. By a further Order, the Appellant-husband was directed to make payment of the arrears towards interim maintenance to the wife and a further amount which was due and payable to the wife towards arrears of maintenance, as per his own admission. By a subsequent Order, it was recorded that only a part of the arrears had been paid. A final opportunity was granted to the Appellant-husband to make payment of the balance amount, failing which, the Court would proceed under the Contempt of Courts Act for wilful disobedience with the Orders passed by this Court. In the backdrop of the facts of this case, it was fit to frame guidelines on certain aspects pertaining to the payment of maintenance in matrimonial matters.

Hon'ble Apex Court held, while dismissing/allowing the appeals:

Held, while disposing off the appeal:

(i) The Judgment and order passed by the Family Court, affirmed by the High Court for payment of interim maintenance to the Respondent No. 1-wife, and Respondent No. 2-son, was affirmed by this Court. The husband was directed to pay the entire arrears of maintenance within a period of twelve weeks from the date of this Judgment, and continue to comply with this Order during the pendency of the proceedings under Section 125 Code of Criminal Procedure before the Family Court. If the Appellant-husband fails to comply with the said directions of this Court, it would be open to the Respondents to have the Order enforced under Section 128 Code of Criminal Procedure, and take recourse to all other remedies which are available in accordance with law.

(ii) To overcome the issue of overlapping jurisdiction, and avoid conflicting orders being passed in different proceedings, it had become necessary to issue directions in this regard, so that there was uniformity in the practice followed by the Family Courts/District Courts/Magistrate Courts throughout the country. It was directed that

(a) where successive claims for maintenance were made by a party under different statutes, the Court would consider an adjustment or set-off, of the amount awarded in the previous proceeding/s, while determining whether any further amount was to be awarded in the subsequent proceeding.

(b) it was made mandatory for the Applicant to disclose the previous proceeding and the orders passed therein, in the subsequent proceeding.

(c) If the order passed in the previous proceeding/s requires any modification or variation, it would be required to be done in the same proceeding.

(iii) The Affidavit of Disclosure of Assets and Liabilities annexed of this judgment, as may be applicable, shall be filed by both parties in all maintenance proceedings, including pending proceedings before the concerned Family Court/District Court/Magistrates Court, as the case may be, throughout the country.

(iv) For determining the quantum of maintenance payable to an applicant, the Court shall take into account the criteria enumerated in Part B - III of the judgment.

(v) The maintenance in all cases will be awarded from the date of filing the application for maintenance.

(vi) For enforcement/execution of orders of maintenance, it was directed that an order or decree of maintenance may be enforced under Section 28A of the Hindu Marriage Act, 1956 (sic1955), Section 20(6) of the D.V. Act and Section 128 of Code of Criminal Procedure, as may be applicable. The order of maintenance may be enforced as a money decree of a civil court as per the provisions of the Code of Civil Procedure, more particularly Sections 51, 55, 58, 60 read with Order 21.

CHAPTER FIVE

KRISHNAVENI RAI VS. PANKAJ RAI AND ORS., 2020

Hon'ble Judges/Coram:

Indira Banerjee and M.R. Shah, JJ.

Relevant Section:

CODE OF CRIMINAL PROCEDURE, 1973 (CRPC) - SECTION 125

No. of pdf pages of Original Judgment : 8

Equivalent citations:

AIR2020SC1156, 2020(4)ALD138, 2020 (2) ALD(Crl.) 180 (SC), 2020(2)ALT91, 2021 (1) ALT (Crl.) 499 (A.P.), 2020(3)BLJ263, 2020(2)CTC359, I(2020)DMC716SC, 2021GLH(1)237, 2020(1)HLR870, 2020(3)J.L.J.R.237, 2020(1)JCC712, 2020(2)JKJ280[SC], 2020(2)JLJ613, 2020 (2) KHC 48, 2020(1)KLJ934, 2020(2)KLT256, 2020(II)OLR224, 2020(3)PLJR169, 2020(2)RCR(Criminal)154, 2020(2)RLW1005(SC), (2020)11SCC253, 2020(2)UC997 MANU/SC/0215/2020

Case Note:

Family - Maintenance - Validity of marriage - Section 125 of Code of Criminal Procedure, 1973 and Section 15 of Hindu Marriage Act, 1955 - Appellant's first marriage was dissolved by decree of divorce and appeal preferred against said decree of divorce after lapse of period of limitation which was condoned - Said appeal was, however, formally dismissed as withdrawn - Thereafter, Appellant married the Respondent No. 1 which also did not work - Appellant lodged complaint against Respondent No. 1 under Sections 406, 498A and 500 of Code - Appellant filed application under Section 125 of Code for maintenance - Respondent No. 1 filed application for discharge, from criminal proceedings initiated against him, which was dismissed - Respondent No. 1 filed criminal Revision Petition against said order - Metropolitan Sessions Judge allowed Criminal Revision Petition and discharged Respondent No. 1 - In meanwhile, Additional Metropolitan Sessions Judge, dismissed application filed by Appellant, claiming maintenance under Section 125 of Code -Appellant filed revision petition in High Court discharging Respondent No. 1 - High Court suspended said order of discharge - Respondent No. 1, filed petition in High Court for quashing of criminal proceedings against him - Said criminal proceedings were quashed on ground that marriage of Appellant with Respondent No. 1, solemnised during pendency of appeal from decree of dissolution of Appellant's marriage with her first husband, was null and void - Revision Petition filed by Appellant against order passed by Additional Metropolitan Sessions Judge dismissing application under Section 125 of Code was also dismissed on same ground on which Criminal proceedings against Respondent No. 1 had been quashed - Hence, present appeal - Whether marriage of Appellant with Respondent No. 1, solemnised during pendency of appeal from decree of dissolution of Appellant's marriage with her first husband, was null and void.

Facts:

The Appellant's first marriage was dissolved by decree of divorce and appeal preferred against said decree of divorce after lapse of period of limitation which was condoned. The said appeal was, however, formally dismissed as withdrawn. Thereafter, the Appellant married the Respondent No. 1, unfortunately, the Appellant's second marriage also did not work. The Appellant had alleged that the Respondent No. 1 subjected the Appellant to harassment and cruelty and even threw her out of the matrimonial home. The Appellant lodged a complaint against the Respondent No. 1 under Sections 406, 498A and 500 of Indian Penal Code. The Appellant filed an application under Section 125 the Code of Criminal Procedure for maintenance. The Respondent No. 1 filed an application under Section 239 for Code of Criminal Procedure for discharge, from the proceedings initiated pursuant to FIR which was dismissed. The Respondent No. 1 filed a criminal Revision Petition in the Court of the Metropolitan Sessions Judge, challenging the said order of Additional Chief Metropolitan Magistrate, rejecting the application of the Respondent No. 1 for discharge. The Metropolitan Sessions Judge, allowed the Criminal

Revision Petition and discharged the Respondent No. 1 from the proceedings Under Section 406, 498A and 500 of the Indian Penal Code. In the meanwhile, the Additional Metropolitan Sessions Judge, dismissed the application filed by the Appellant, claiming maintenance under Section 125 Code of Criminal Procedure. The Appellant filed a Criminal Revision Petition in the High Court inter alia challenging the order discharging the Respondent No. 1 from the proceeding under Sections 406, 498A and 500 of the Indian Penal Code and also made an application for suspension of the said order of discharge. By an order, the High Court suspended the said order of discharge. The Respondent No. 1, on the other hand, filed a petition under Section 482 of the Code of Criminal Procedure, for quashing of the criminal proceedings against him. The said criminal proceedings were quashed on the ground that the marriage of the Appellant with the Respondent No. 1, solemnised during the pendency of an appeal from the decree of dissolution of the Appellant's marriage with her first husband, was null and void. The Criminal Revision Petition filed by the Appellant against the order passed by the Additional Metropolitan Sessions Judge dismissing the application under Section 125 of the Code of Criminal Procedure was also dismissed by an order on the same ground on which the Criminal proceedings against the Respondent No. 1 had been quashed.

Hon'ble Apex Court held, while dismissing/allowing the appeals:

Held, while allowing the appeal:

(i) The bar, if any, under Section 15 of the Hindu Marriage Act applies only if there is an appeal filed within the period of limitation, and not afterwards upon condonation of delay in filing an appeal unless of course, the decree of divorce is stayed or there is an interim order of Court, restraining the parties or any of them from remarrying during the pendency of the appeal.

(ii) The appeal was infructuous for all practical purposes, from the inception, since the Appellant's ex-husband had lawfully remarried after expiry of the period of limitation for filing an appeal, there being no appeal till then.

(iii) It could never have been the legislative intent that a marriage validly contracted after the divorce and after expiry of the period of limitation to file an appeal from the decree of divorce should rendered void on the filing of a belated appeal. If the marriage of the Appellant's ex-husband was a valid marriage in law recognizing that he had no living spouse, the subsequent re-marriage of the Appellant could also not be void. We are in full agreement with the view of this Court in Leela Gupta that the effect of the prohibition against one of the parties from contracting a second marriage for a certain period is not to nullify the divorce and continue the dissolved marriage, as if the same were subsisting.

(iv) The judgment and order under appeal confirming the order dismissing the application under Section 125 of Code by relying on the order in Criminal Petition could not be sustained.

Disposition:

Appeal Allowed

CHAPTER SIX

ABHILASHA VS. PARKASH AND ORS., 2020

Hon'ble Judges/Coram:

Ashok Bhushan, R. Subhash Reddy and M.R. Shah, JJ.

Relevant Section:

CODE OF CRIMINAL PROCEDURE, 1973 (CRPC) - SECTION 125; HINDU ADOPTIONS AND MAINTANCE ACT, 1956 – SECTION 20

No. of pdf pages of Original Judgment : 14

Equivalent citations:

2020(214)AIC10, AIR2020SC4355, 2020 (2) ALD(Crl.) 987 (SC), 2020ALLMR(Cri)4047, 2020 (143) ALR 189, 2020 (3) ALT (Crl.) 255 (A.P.), 2020(5)BLJ517, 2021 (1) CCC 162 , 2021(1)CGLJ240, 2020CriLJ4770, 2021(1)Crimes185(SC), 2020(6)CTC198, III(2020)DMC265SC, 2020(3)HLR290, ILR2020(4)Kerala85, 2020(4)J.L.J.R.129, 2020(5)JKJ105[SC], 2020(4)KCCR2698, 2020 (5) KHC 235, 2020(4)KLJ814, 2020(6)KLT341, 2021-2-LW134, 2021-1-LW(Crl)333, 2020(4)MLJ(Crl)95, 2020(II)OLR692, 2020(4)PLJR87, 2020(4)RCR(Criminal)141, 2021 150 RD113, 2020 (9-10) SCJ 154, 2020(2)UC1363 MANU/SC/0683/2020

Case Note:

Criminal - Maintenance - Section 125 of the Code of Criminal Procedure, 1973 (CrPC) -Respondent No.2 claimed maintenance for herself, her two sons and Appellant daughter - All applications except Appellant dismissed by Trial Court - Appellant was allowed maintenance till she attains majority - Revision filed against thereto was dismissed followed by dismissal of petition under Section 482, CrPC by the High Court vide impugned judgment - Hence, the present appeal - Appellant submitted that even though the Appellant had o?=attained o?=majority on but since she is unmarried, she is entitled to claim maintenance from her father - (i) Whether the Appellant entitled to claim maintenance from her father in proceedings under Section =125 =CrPC although not suffering from any physical or mental abnormality/injury? - (ii) Whether orders limiting the claim of the Appellant to claim maintenance till she attains majority deserves to be set aside with direction to the Respondent No. 1 to continue to give maintenance till she remains unmarried?

Facts:

The Respondent No. 2, mother of the Appellant, on her behalf, as well as on behalf of her two sons and the Appellant daughter, filed an application under Section 125 of the Code of Criminal Procedure against her husband, the Respondent No. 1, claiming maintenance for herself and her three children. The application of the Applicant Nos. 1, 2 and 3 was dismissed and that of the Applicant No. 4 (Appellant) was allowed till she attains majority. All the four applicants filed a criminal revision, which was dismissed with the only modification that Appellant would be entitled to maintenance till the date she attains majority. High Court by the impugned judgment dismissed the application filed under Section 482 of the Code of Criminal Procedure by observing that both the Courts were consistent with regard to declining maintenance to Petitioners No. 1 to 3. As regards grant of maintenance to Appellant it was observed that there was no illegality or infirmity and accordingly the petition was dismissed. Hence, the present Appeal. It was contended that High Court committed error in dismissing the application of the Appellant on wrong premise that since she has attained majority and not suffering from any physical or mental abnormality, is not entitled for any maintenance

Hon'ble Apex Court held, while dismissing/allowing the appeals:

Held, while dismissing the Appeals:

i. The provision of Section 20 of Act, 1956 cast clear statutory obligation on a Hindu to maintain his unmarried daughter who is unable to maintain herself. The right of unmarried daughter under Section 20 to claim maintenance from her father when she is unable to maintain herself is absolute and the right given to unmarried daughter under Section 20 is right granted under personal law, which can very well be enforced by her against her father.

ii. In the instant case, the Magistrate while deciding proceedings under Section 125 Code of Criminal Procedure could not have exercised the jurisdiction under Section 20(3) of Act, 1956 and the submission of the Appellant cannot be accepted that the Court below should have allowed the application for maintenance even though she has become major. There was no infirmity in the order of the Judicial Magistrate First Class as well as learned Additional Magistrate in not granting maintenance to Appellant who had become major.

iii. The purpose and object of Section 125 Code of Criminal Procedure is to provide immediate relief to applicant in a summary proceedings, whereas right under Section 20 read with Section 3(b) of Act, 1956 contains larger right, which needs determination by a Civil Court, hence for the larger claims as enshrined under Section 20, the proceedings need to be initiated under Section 20 of the Act and the legislature never contemplated to burden the Magistrate while exercising jurisdiction under Section 125 Code of Criminal Procedure to determine the claims contemplated by Act, 1956.

iv. There are three more reasons due to which we are satisfied that the orders passed by the learned Judicial Magistrate as well as learned Additional Sessions Judge in the revision was not required to be interfered with by the High Court in exercise of jurisdiction under Section 482 Code of Criminal Procedure: (i) The application was filed by the mother of the Appellant in the year 2002 claiming maintenance on her behalf as well as on behalf of her two sons and Appellant, who was minor at that time. The Appellant being minor at that time when application was filed on 17.10.2002, there was no occasion for any pleading on behalf of the Appellant that she was not able to maintain herself even after attaining the majority. Section 20 of the Act, 1956 on which reliance has been placed by learned Counsel for the Appellant recognising the right of maintenance of unmarried daughter by a person subject to the condition when "the parents or the unmarried daughter, as the case may be, is unable to maintain themselves/herself out of their/her own earnings or other property". The learned Additional Sessions Judge noticed the submission of the Respondent that Appellant did not come in the witness box even when she had attained majority to claim that she was unable to maintain herself; (ii) From the judgment of the learned Judicial Magistrate, another fact, which is relevant to be noticed is that applicant Nos. 2 to 4, which included the Appellant also had filed the proceedings under Section 20 of the Act, 1956 being Suit No. 6 of 2001, which was dismissed as withdrawn on 17.12.2012;

(iii) Another factor, which need to be noticed that in the counter affidavit filed in this appeal, there was a specific pleading of the Respondent that a plot of land was purchased in name of the Appellant admeasuring 214 sq. Yds. In the rejoinder affidavit filed by the Appellant, it has been admitted that the plot was purchased on 31.07.2000 from the joint income earned by mother and father of the Appellant, which had been agreed to be sold in the year 2012 for a total sale consideration of Rs. 11,77,000/-. In the rejoinder affidavit, an affidavit of prospective purchaser has been filed by the Appellant, where it is mentioned that agreement to sell had taken place between Appellant and Arjun on 31.07.2000 for a sale consideration of Rs. 11,77,000/-, out of which Appellant had received Rs. 10,89,000 as earnest money

v. It was accepted as a preposition of law that an unmarried Hindu daughter can claim maintenance from her father till she is married relying on Section 20(3) of the Act, 1956, provided she pleads and proves that she is unable to maintain herself, for enforcement of which right her application/ suit has to be under Section 20 of Act, 1956.

vi. In facts of the present case the ends of justice be served by giving liberty to the Appellant to take recourse to Section 20(3) of the Act, 1956, if so advised, for claiming any maintenance against her father. Subject to liberty as above, the appeal was dismissed.

Disposition:

Appeal Dismissed

CHAPTER SEVEN

KAMALA AND ORS. VS M.R. MOHAN KUMAR, 2018

Hon'ble Judges/Coram:

R. Banumathi and Indira Banerjee, JJ.

Relevant Section:

CRIMINAL MATTERS - MATTERS RELATING TO MAINTENANCE UNDER SECTION 125 OF CR.P.C.

No. of pdf pages of Original Judgment: 7

Equivalent citations:

2018(3)ACR3145, 2018(192)AIC263, AIR2018SC5128, 2019 (1) ALD(Crl.) 262 (SC), 2019 (106) ACC 651, 2019 (132) ALR 200, 2019 (1) ALT (Crl.) 65 (A.P.), IV(2018)CCR355(SC), 2018(4)Crimes382(SC), III(2018)DMC694SC, 2019(1)HLR62, 2018(4)J.L.J.R.357, 2018(4)JKJ14[SC], 2018 (5) KHC 914, 2018(4)KLT864, 2019-2-LW277, 2019-1-LW(Crl)434, 2018(II)OLR994, 2018(4)PLJR362, 2018(4)RCR(Criminal)894, 2018(14)SCALE257, (2019)11SCC491, 2018(3)UC2044 MANU/SC/1203/2018

Case Note:

Family - Maintenance - Section 125 Code of Criminal Procedure, 1973 (CrPC) - Present appeals arose out of judgment passed by High Court by which High Court had set aside judgment of family Court which had directed Respondent to pay maintenance to Appellants-wife and children - Whether high Court was right in holding that, Appellant was not entitled for any maintenance.

Facts:

Appellant No. 1 filed a Criminal Miscellaneous No. 297/2006 under Section 125 of CrPC claiming maintenance for herself and children from Respondent as she could not maintain herself and her children. Upon consideration of evidence, family Court held that, Appellant No. 1 had proved that there was husband-wife relationship between Appellant No. 1 and Respondent and that Appellants No. 2 and 3 are children born out of said wedlock and that Respondent was giving her a monthly maintenance of 3,000/- per month. The family court further held that, case of Appellants was supported by evidence of PW-2 and PW-3 which clearly establish that, they lived under same roof and society also accepted them as husband and wife. Family Court vide its order allowed the Appellant's claim. In appeal, High Court had set aside order of family Court and held that Appellant No. 1 was unable to prove that she was legally wedded wife of Respondent. High Court further held that, she had not produced any evidence to show that, marriage was solemnized as per custom and she, not being legally wedded wife, was not entitled for any maintenance.

Hon'ble Apex Court held, while dismissing/allowing the appeals:

Held, while allowing the appeals

It was fairly well settled that, law presumed in favour of marriage and against concubinage when a man and woman had cohabited continuously for a number of years.

On basis of evidence of Appellant No. 1 (PW-1), birth certificates of Appellant Nos. 2 and 3 (Exts. P7-P8 dated 25.05.2001 and 06.08.2003), other documentary evidence, oral evidence of PW-2 who was co-worker of Appellant No. 1 and PW-3-landlord, the family court held that Appellant No. 1 and the Respondent were living together as husband and wife and there is sufficient proof of marriage. The family court rightly drew the presumption of valid marriage between Appellant No. 1 and the Respondent and that they are legally married couple for claiming maintenance by the wife under Section 125 of CrPC which is summary in nature. The evidence of PW-1 coupled with the birth certificates of Appellants No. 2 and 3 and other evidences clearly establish the factum of marriage.

Based upon oral and documentary evidence, when the family Court held that, there was a valid marriage, High Court being revisional Court had no power re-assessing evidence and substitute its views on findings of fact. High Court did not keep in view that in proceedings under Section 125 of CrPC, strict proof of marriage was not necessary. Findings recorded by family Court as to existence of a valid marriage ought not to have been interfered with by High Court.

Impugned judgment of High Court was set aside and appeals allowed. The Respondent shall pay arrears of maintenance as directed by the family Court, Mysore to the Appellants within a period of two months. Additionally, the Respondent shall also continue to pay the maintenance to the Appellants as directed by the family court on or before 10th of every English calendar month. The Appellants are also at liberty to move the family court for enhancement of the maintenance.

Disposition:

Appeal Allowed

CHAPTER EIGHT

SHAMIM BANO VS. ASRAF KHAN, 2014

Hon'ble Judges/Coram:

Dipak Misra and Vikramajit Sen, JJ.

Relevant Section:

INDIAN PENAL CODE, 1860 (IPC) - SECTION 498A; CODE OF CRIMINAL PROCEDURE, 1973 (CRPC) - SECTION 125; CODE OF CRIMINAL CODE, 1973 (CRPC) –

No. of pdf pages of Original Judgment : 7

Equivalent citations:

2014(2)ACR1857(SC), 2014v AD (S.C.) 94, 2014(138)AIC267, 2014 (85) ACC 964, 2014ALLMR(Cri)2200, 2014 (105) ALR 228, 2014(3)BomCR(Cri)10, III(2014)CCR522(SC), 2014(2)Crimes234(SC), 2014(2)HLR129, 2014(3)J.L.J.R.201, JT2014(6)SC393, 2014(3)KLJ148, 2014(2)N.C.C.133, 2014(3)PLJR139, 2014(2)RCR(Civil)820, 2014(2)RCR(Criminal)592, 2014(5)SCALE299, (2014)12SCC636, 2015 (9) SCJ 477, 2015(1)ShimLC197 MANU/SC/0332/2014

Case Note:

Code of Criminal Procedure, 1973 - Section 125--Maintenance-Grant of maintenance in favour of divorced Muslim woman--Even if application filed under Section 3 of Muslim Woman (Protection of Rights on Divorce) Act, 1986--Magistrate under aforesaid Act has power to grant maintenance in favour of divorced Muslim woman--Parameters and considerations are same as stipulated in Section 125--Magistrate could exercise power under Section 125 for grant of maintenance in favour of divorced Muslim woman under aforesaid Act--Judgment and order of High Court--Set aside--Matter remitted to Magistrate for re-adjudication of controversy in question.

Facts:

While the application for grant of maintenance was pending, divorce between the appellant and the respondent took place on 5.5.1997. At that juncture, the appellant filed Criminal Case No. 56 of 1997 under Section 3 of the Muslim Women (Protection of Rights on Divorce) Act. 1986 (for brevity "the Act") before the learned Judicial Magistrate First Class, Durg. The learned Magistrate, who was hearing the application preferred under Section 125 of the Code, dismissed the same on 14.7.1999 on the ground that the appellant had not been able to prove cruelty and had been living separately and hence, she was not entitled to get the benefit of maintenance. The learned Magistrate, while dealing with the application preferred under Section 3 of the Act, allowed the application directing the husband and others to pay a sum of ` 11,786 towards mahr, return of goods and ornaments and a sum of ` 1,750 towards maintenance during the Iddat period.

Before the High Court a preliminary objection was raised on behalf of the respondent-husband that the petition under Section 125 of the Code was not maintainable by a divorced woman without complying with the provisions contained in Section 5 of the Act. It was further put forth that initial action under Section 125 of the Code by the appellant-wife was tenable but the same deserved to be thrown overboard after she had filed an application under Section 3 of the Act for return of gifts and properties, for payment of mahr and also for grant of maintenance during the 'Iddat' period. It was also urged that the wife was only entitled to maintenance during the Iddat period and the same having been granted in the application, which was filed after the divorce, grant of any maintenance did not arise in exercise of power under Section 125 of the Code. The two seminal issues that emanate for consideration are, first whether the appellant's application for grant of maintenance under Section 125 of the Code is to be restricted to the date of divorce and, as an ancillary to it because of filing of an application under Section 3 of the Act after the divorce for grant of mahr and return of gifts would disentitle the appellant to sustain the application under Section 125 of the Code; and second, whether regard being had to the present fact situation, as observed by the High Court, the consent under Section 5 of the Act was an imperative to maintain the application.

Hon'ble Apex Cssourt held, while dismissing/allowing the appeals:

Held, even an application has been filed under the provisions of the Act, the Magistrate under the Act has the power to grant maintenance in favour of a divorced Muslim woman and the parameters and the considerations are the same as stipulated in Section 125 of the Code.

CHAPTER NINE

Badshah Vs. Urmila Badshah Godse and Ors., 2013

Hon'ble Judges/Coram:

Ranjana Prakash Desai and A.K. Sikri, JJ

Relevant Section:

CODE OF CRIMINAL PROCEDURE, 1973 (CrPC) - Section 125; CODE OF CRIMINAL PROCEDURE, 1973 (CrPC)

No. of pdf pages of Original Judgment : 9

Equivalent citations:

2013(3)ACR3010, 2013XI AD (S.C.) 9, 2013(132)AIC108, AIR2014SC869, 2013 (101) ALR 704, 2013(4)BLJ233, 2013BomCR(Cri)616, 2013(4)BomCR(Cri)616, IV(2013)CCR541(SC), 2014CriLJ1076, III(2013)DMC518, 2014GLH(1)273, 2013(2)HLR732, 2014(1)J.L.J.R.78, 2013(4)JCC2765, JT2013(13)SC570, 2013(4)KLT367, 2014-2-LW936, 2014-1-LW(Crl)646, 2014(2)MPHT499, 2014(1)N.C.C.238, 2014(1)PLJR144, 2013(4)RCR(Civil)830, 2013(4)RCR(Criminal)764, 2013(4)RLW3670(SC), 2013(12)SCALE681, (2014)1SCC188, 2014 (2) SCJ 779 MANU/SC/1084/2013

Case Note:

(1) Code of Criminal Procedure, 1973 - Section 125--Maintenance to wife and daughter--Question involved--Whether in any case respondent No. 1 could be treated as "wife" of petitioner as he was already married and therefore petition under Section 125 at her instance was maintainable?--Respondent No. 1 able to prove by cogent and strong evidence, that petitioner and respondent No. 1 married each

other--Marriage between parties--Proved--However, petitioner (husband) was already married--But he duped respondent No. 1 by suppressing factum of alleged first marriage--When marriage between respondent No. 1 and petitioner was solemnized, petitioner kept respondent No. 1 in dark about his first surviving marriage--False representation was given to respondent No. 1 that he was single and was competent to enter into marital tie with respondent No. 1--Held--In such circumstances, petitioner cannot be permitted to deny benefit of maintenance to respondent No. 1, taking advantage of his own wrong and turn around to say that respondents are not entitled to maintenance under Section 125 as respondent No. 1 is not "legally wedded wife" of the petitioner.

Facts:

At least for purpose of Section 125, respondent No. 1 would be treated as "legally wedded wife" of petitioner--In such cases, purposive interpretation needs to be given to provisions of Section 125--Impugned order of High Court affirming award of maintenance to respondents by trial court requires no interference. The facts emerging on record in the instant case would reveal that at the time when the petitioner married the respondent No. 1, he had living wife and the said marriage was still subsisting. Therefore, under the provisions of Hindu Marriage Act, the petitioner could not have married second time. At the same time, it has also come on record that the petitioner duped respondent No. 1 by not revealing the fact of his first marriage and pretending that he was single. After this marriage both lived together and respondent No. 2 was also born from this wedlock. In such circumstances, whether respondents could file application under Section 125 of the Cr.P.C., is the issue. In the present case, respondent No. 1 has been able to prove, by cogent and strong evidence, that the petitioner and respondent No. 1 had been married each other. When the marriage between respondent No. 1 and petitioner was solemnized, the petitioner had kept the respondent No. 1 in dark about his first marriage, A false representation was given to respondent No. 1 that he was single and was competent to enter into marital tie with respondent No. 1. In such circumstances, can the petitioner be allowed to take advantage of his own wrong and turn around to say that respondents are not entitled to maintenance by filing the petition under Section 125, Cr.P.C. as respondent No. 1 is not "legally wedded wife" of the petitioner? The present case is a case where the marriage between the parties has been proved. However, the petitioner was already married. But he duped the respondent by suppressing the factum of alleged first marriage. On these facts, he cannot be permitted to deny the benefit of maintenance to the respondent, taking advantage of his own wrong. In such cases, purposive interpretation needs to be given to the provisions of Section 125, Cr.P.C.If this interpretation is not accepted, it would amount to giving a premium to the husband for defrauding the wife. Therefore, at least for the purpose of claiming maintenance under Section 125, Cr.P.C. such a woman is to be treated as the legally wedded wife.(2) Interpretation of Statute--If choice is between two interpretations--Narrower of which would fail to achieve manifest purpose of legislation should be avoided--Court to avoid construction which would reduce legislation to futility and should accept bolder construction based on view that Parliament would legislate only for purpose of bringing about effective result--While interpreting statute court may not only take into consideration purpose for which statute was enacted--But also mischief it seeks to suppress.(3) Interpretation of Statute--Provisions of Section 125 of Cr.P.C.--Purposive interpretation needs to be given to provisions of Section 125 of Cr.P.C

Hon'ble Apex Court held, while dismissing/allowing the appeals:

It is further held:

It is to be remembered that the order passed in an application under Section 125 Code of Criminal Procedure does not finally determine the rights and obligations of the parties and the said section is enacted with a view to provide summary remedy for providing maintenance to a wife, children and parents. For the purpose of getting his rights determined, the Appellant has also filed Civil Suit which is spending before the trial court.

Provision of maintenance would definitely fall in this category which aims at empowering the destitute and achieving social justice or equality and dignity of the individual. While dealing with cases under this provision, drift in the approach from "adversarial" litigation to social context adjudication is the need of the hour.

The brooding presence of the Constitutional empathy for the weaker sections like women and children must inform interpretation if it has to have social relevance. So viewed, it is possible to be selective in picking out that interpretation out of two alternatives which advances the cause - the cause of the derelicts.

For the aforesaid reasons, we are not inclined to grant leave and dismiss this petition.

CHAPTER TEN

SHAMIMA FAROOQUI VS. SHAHID KHAN, 2015

Hon'ble Judges/Coram:

Dipak Misra and Prafulla C. Pant, JJ.

Relevant Section:

CRIMINAL MATTERS - MATTERS RELATING TO MAINTENANCE UNDER SECTION 125 OF CR.P.C.

No. of pdf pages of the Original Judgment : 7

Equivalent citations:

2015IV AD (S.C.) 301, AIR2015SC2025, 2015(4)AJR627, 2015(2) AKR 758, 2015 (2) ALD(Crl.) 549 (SC), 2015 (90) ACC 43, 2015ALLMR(Cri)2046, 2015 (2) ALT (Crl.) 419 (SC), 2015(2)BLJ167, 2015(2)BomCR(Cri)289, II(2015)CCR205(SC), 2015CriLJ2551, 2015(2)Crimes133(SC), 2015(3)CTC80, 2015(2)HLR232, 2015(2)J.L.J.R.476, 2015(2)JCC1285, 2015(2)KLJ202, 2015-4-LW106, 2015-2-LW(Crl)224, (2015) 2 MLJ(Crl) 237 (SC), 2015(2)N.C.C.282, 2015(II)OLR(SC)68, 2015(3)PLJR58, (2015)178PLR696, 2015(2)RCR(Civil)628, 2015(2)RCR(Criminal)526, 2015(2)RLW1769(SC), 2015(4)SCALE521, (2015)5SCC705, 2015 (5) SCJ 342 MANU/SC/0380/2015

Case Notes:

Criminal - Reduction of maintenance - Delay in disposal - Section 125 of Code of Criminal Procedure, 1973 - High Court modified awarded maintenance by holding that Family Court had not ascribed any reason for grant of maintenance - Hence, present appeal - Whether High Court rightly held that grant of maintenance was excessive and reduced it from date of retirement of Respondent-husband till marriage of Appellant-wife -

Held, Section 125 of Code had been rightly held to be applicable by Family Judge - Though application for grant of maintenance was filed, it was not decided for more than decade - There was no order for grant of interim maintenance - When application for grant of maintenance was filed by wife delay in disposal of application, to say least, was unacceptable situation - High Court had shown immense sympathy to husband by reducing amount after his retirement - Wife was entitled to lead life in similar manner as she would have lived in house of her husband - Obligation of husband was on higher pedestal when question of maintenance of wife and children arose - Solely because husband had retired, there was no justification to reduce maintenance by its half - Impugned order set aside and order of Family Court restored - Appeal allowed.

Facts:

The facts which are requisite to be stated for adjudication of these appeals are that the Appellant filed an application Under Section 125 of the Code of Criminal Procedure (Code of Criminal Procedure) contending, *inter alia*, that she married Shahid Khan, the Respondent herein, on 26.4.1992 and during her stay at the matrimonial home she was prohibited from talking to others, and the husband not only demanded a car from the family but also started harassing her. A time came when he sent her to the parental home where she was compelled to stay for almost three months. The indifferent husband did not come to take her back to the matrimonial home, but she returned with the fond and firm hope that the bond of wedlock would be sustained and cemented with love and peace but as the misfortune would have it, the demand for the vehicle continued and the harassment was used as a weapon for fulfilment of the demand. In due course she came to learn that the husband had illicit relationship with another woman and he wanted to marry her. Usual to sense of human curiosity and wife's right when she asked him she was assaulted. The situation gradually worsened and it became unbearable for her to stay at the matrimonial home. At that juncture, she sought help of her parents who came and took her to the parental home at Lucknow where she availed treatment. Being deserted and ill-treated and, in a way, suffering from fear psychosis she took shelter in the house of her parents and when all her hopes got shattered for reunion, she filed an application for grant of maintenance at the rate of Rs. 4000/- per month on the foundation that husband was working on the post of Nayak in the Army and getting a salary of Rs. 10,000/- approximately apart from other perks.

Hon'ble Apex Court held, while dismissing/allowing the appeals:

Leave granted.

In the instant case, as is seen, the High Court has reduced the amount of maintenance from Rs. 4,000/- to Rs. 2,000/-. As is manifest, the High Court has become oblivious of the fact that she has to stay on her own. Needless to say, the order of the learned Family Judge is not manifestly perverse. There is nothing perceptible which would show that order is a sanctuary of errors. In fact, when the order is based on proper appreciation of evidence on record, no revisional court should have interfered with the reason on the base that it would have arrived at a different or another conclusion. When substantial justice has been done, there was no reason to interfere. There may be a shelter over her head in the parental house, but other real expenses cannot be ignored. Solely because the husband had retired, there was no justification to reduce the maintenance by 50%. It is not a huge fortune that was showered on the wife that it deserved reduction. It only reflects the non-application of mind and, therefore, we are unable to sustain the said order.

The aforesaid aspects have gone uncontroverted as the Respondent -husband has not appeared and contested the matter. Therefore, we are disposed to accept the assertions. This exposition of facts further impels us to set aside the order of the High Court.

Consequently, the appeals are allowed, the orders passed by the High Court are set aside and that of the Family Court is restored. There shall be no order as to costs.

CHAPTER ELEVEN

Sau Shaila Balasaheb Kadam Vs. Balasaheb Hindurao Kadam, 2014

Hon'ble Judges/Coram:

SV. Gopala Gowda and C. Nagappan, JJ.

Relevant Section:

CODE OF CRIMINAL PROCEDURE, 1973 (CrPC) - Section 125; HINDU ADOPTIONS AND MAINTENANCE ACT, 1956 - Section 18(2)

No. of pdf pages of the Original Judgment: 3

Equivalent citations:

2015 (110) ALR 406, 2015(1)ALT44(SC), 2014 6 AWC6027SC, 2015(1)BomCR113, 2014 (4) CCC 262 , I(2015)DMC758SC, 2015(1)HLR193, 2015(1)J.L.J.R.6, 2015(4)MhLJ173(SC), 2015MPLJ483(SC), 2015(1)PLJR232, 2014(4)RCR(Civil)1024, 2014(4)RCR(Criminal)947, 2015 128 RD286, 2014(12)SCALE646, (2015)1SCC802, 2014 (10) SCJ 166, (2015)2WBLR(SC)1, 2014 (4) WLN 165 (SC) MANU/SC/1006/2014

Case Notes:

Family - Claim for maintenance - Substantial question of law - Consideration thereof - Section 18 of Hindu Adoptions and Maintenance Act, 1956 - High Court held that Appellant had married 1st Respondent during subsistence of his earlier marriage and therefore, she was not entitled to claim any maintenance under Section 18 of Act - Hence, present appeal - Whether High Court held that there was no substantial question of law which required its consideration - Held, High Court though recorded submissions made by both sides, had not dealt with same in proper perspective in impugned order - It was obvious recent decision of present Court referred to was not available to High Court at that time - However, rejection of Appellant's claim on ground of having no substantial question of law arising for consideration, was not proper - Without expressing any opinion on merits of contentions raised, matter was remanded back to High Court for fresh consideration - Impugned order set aside - Appeal allowed.

Facts:

The trial court framed six issues and witnesses were examined on both sides and it held that though the Appellant/Plaintiff is the second wife, she is entitled to maintenance amount of Rs. 450/- per month from her husband, and decreed the suit accordingly by creating a charge on the suit properties for the said amount. Respondent No. 1 herein/husband preferred appeal and the appellate court held that the Plaintiff being second wife, she is not entitled to claim maintenance and allowed the appeal by setting aside the judgment of the trial court and the suit came to be dismissed. The Appellant herein/Plaintiff preferred the second appeal and the High Court held that the Appellant had married the Respondent No. 1 during the subsistence of his earlier marriage and hence she is not entitled to claim any maintenance Under Section 18 of the Hindu Adoptions and Maintenance Act, 1956, and rejected the second appeal by holding that there is no substantial question of law which requires its consideration. Challenging the same the present appeals have been preferred.

Hon'ble Apex Court held, while dismissing/allowing the appeals:

The High Court though recorded the submissions made by the counsel on both sides, have not dealt with the same in proper perspective in the impugned judgment of course the recent decision of this Court referred to supra was not available to the High Court at the time of disposal of the second appeal. However, the rejection of the same on the ground of having no substantial question of law arising for consideration, in our view is not proper and the judgment is liable to be set aside. Without expressing any opinion on the merits of the contentions raised, we deem it fit to remit the matter to the High Court for fresh consideration.

CHAPTER TWELVE

SAYGO BAI VS. CHUEERU BAJRANGI, 2010

Hon'ble Judges/Coram:

V.S. Sirpurkar and T.S. Thakur, JJ.

Relevant Section:

CODE OF CRIMINAL PROCEDURE, 1973 (CrPC) - Section 125

No. of pdf pages of the Original Judgement: 6

Equivalent citations:

2011(1)ACR1136(SC), 2010(96)AIC17, AIR2011SC1557, 2010 (71) ACC 933, (2011)2CALLT58(SC), 2011CriLJ1007, 2010(4)Crimes340(SC), II(2010)DMC871SC, JT2011(1)SC207, 2011(1)N.C.C.163, 2011(I)OLR(SC)353, 2011(2)PLJR103, 2011(1)RCR(Civil)280, 2011(1)RCR(Criminal)117, RLW2011(3)SC1957, 2010(12)SCALE229, (2010)13SCC762, (2011)2SCC(Cri)415, 2011(1)UC89 MANU/SC/0963/2010

Case Notes :

Criminal Procedure Code, 1973-- Section 125--Maintenance--Denied--Validity--Held--Since the husband admitted second wife and tried to justify it than the finding of lower court that wife has lost the right of maintenance as she is wilful neglecting the husband is erroneous--Set aside the judgment--Allowed the maintenance from the date of application.

Facts:

The appellant Saygo Bai, wife of Chueeru Bajrangi along with her two minor children Jivti (daughter) and Basant (son) filed an application under Section 125 Code of Criminal Procedure against her husband Chueeru

Bajrangi. She pointed out therein that her husband had taken a second wife, namely, one Smt. Gulab Bai and that he was a salaried employee in a Government department. However, he was neglecting to maintain Saygo Bai and her two children. She also pleaded that she had cordial relationship with her husband upto year 1989. However, the respondent-husband started avoiding the family. During the year 1990, he took Gulab Bai as his second wife. As a result, the appellant and her children were thrown out. She claimed the maintenance of Rs. 3,000/- per person per head. The respondent-husband resisted this application claiming that he always maintained good relations with Saygo Bai and used to visit his village Chalani, where his wife and children resided with his parents, off and on. He claimed that when Basant, the younger child was only six months old, Saygo Bai left her matrimonial house without any rhyme or reason and went to her father's place at village Banda. He further pleaded that he tried to bring back the appellant and had gone to that village along with one Shobha and Haria of his village but she refused to come back. All this, according to him, happened five years prior to the second marriage which he had performed for taking care of his two children. In short, he claimed that two children were always with husband and, therefore, there was no question of abandoning them. The claim of the respondent-husband was that the wife left his company without any rhyme or reason. He then pointed out that it was only after five years of abandonment of matrimonial house that his wife Saygo Bai had filed the application for maintenance under Section 125 Code of Criminal Procedure thereby he further pointed out that she was not entitled to any maintenance as she had left his company without any justification.

Hon'ble Apex Court held, while dismissing/allowing the appeals:

We hold that the orders of the Courts below are wholly incorrect. Firstly, the Courts erred in holding that she left the matrimonial house for 4-5 years and refused to join the company of her husband and, secondly, the Courts are totally in error in holding that on that count she has lost the right of maintenance. In our opinion, the application, at least insofar as the appellant was concerned, was liable to be allowed. We allow that application.

Ordinarily, we would have remanded the matter for deciding the amount of maintenance. However, considering that the appellant is in the state of penury and not getting even the interim maintenance, we proceed to decide that issue ourselves. The appellant in her evidence has claimed that the respondent-husband drew a monthly salary of Rs. 2,000/- in the year 1993. Besides, he also had 20 acres of land and grew 40 quintals of Paddy crop, 10 quintals of Wheat crop, 4 quintals of Urad and Rawa crops and Corns etc. There is not even a word of cross-examination on these claims and these claims have gone unchallenged. Even in his own evidence, the respondent has not uttered even a word regarding his salary and has merely claimed that Saygo Bai was maintaining herself by working as a labourer and earned Rs. 45 per day. He made a bald statement that there was no immovable property in his name. He had also categorically admitted that after coming out of the matrimonial house he never maintained Saygo Bai. Considering, therefore, the overall situation, it is obvious that the respondent must be earning at least Rs. 10,000/- per month presently as salary being a Constable in police force and also has other sources of income from agricultural properties. In that view, we are of the opinion that maintenance at the rate of Rs. 1,500/- per month in favour of the appellant would be a proper maintenance. The maintenance shall be payable from the date of the application. The three orders passed by the Courts below are set aside. The appeal is allowed in the above terms.

CHAPTER THIRTEEN

NAGENDRAPPA NATIKAR VS. NEELAMMA, 2013

Hon'ble Judges/Coram:

K.S. Panicker Radhakrishnan and Dipak Misra, JJ.

Relevant Section:

CODE OF CRIMINAL PROCEDURE, 1973 (CrPC) - SECTION 125; INDIAN CONTRACT ACT, 1872 - SECTION 25; HINDU ADOPTION AND MAINTANCE ACT, 1956 - SECTION 18(2)

No. of pdf pages of the Original Judgment : 5

Equivalent citations:

2013(3)ABR420, 2013(125)AIC198, AIR2013SC1541, 2013(2)AJR487, 2013(2) AKR 370, 2013(4)ALD59, 2013(2)ALLMR(SC)952, 2013 (98) ALR 699, 2013(2)ALT61, 2013(3)BomCR616, (2013)3CALLT1(SC), 2013(4)CDR901(SC), 2013(3)CHN189, 116(2013)CLT389, 2013CriLJ2060, 2013(2)CTC440, II(2013)DMC68, 2013(2)HLR205, ILR2013(2)Kerala659, JT2013(4)SC120, 2013(3)KCCR2257, 2013-3-LW776, 2013(II)MPJR225, 2013(II)OLR69, (2013)172PLR55, 2013(2)RCR(Civil)469, 2013(2)RCR(Criminal)424, 2013(2)RLW1350(SC), 2013(3)SCALE561, (2014)14SCC452, [2013]2SCR426, 2013(3)UC2002, (2013)3WBLR(SC)473, 2013(2)WLN38 MANU/SC/0248/2013

Case Notes:

Hindu Adoption and Maintenance Act, 1956 - Section 18--Civil Procedure Code, 1908--Order 23 Rule 3--Criminal Procedure Code, 1973--Section 125/127--Maintenance--Maintainability of suit--Held--Suit under

Section 18 of Act 1956 for maintenance is perfectly maintainable inspite of compromise reached between the parties under Order 23 Rule 3 C.P.C. and accepted by court. Criminal Procedure Code, 1973 - Section 125/127--Proceedings under--Scope--Held--Section 125 of Cr.P.C. is a piece of Social legislation which provides for a summary and speedy relief by way of maintenance--Order made under Section 125 Cr.P.C. is tentative and is subject to final determination of rights of parties in a Civil Suit.

Facts:

Alleging that the Petitioner is not maintaining his wife, Respondent filed an application Under Section 125 Code of Criminal Procedure for grant of maintenance before the 1st Additional JMFC at Gulbarga, being Misc. Case No. 234 of 1992. While the matter was pending, an application was preferred by the parties under Order XXIII Rule 3 Code of Civil Procedure on 3.9.1994 stating that the parties had arrived at a compromise, by which the Respondent had agreed to receive an amount of Rs. 8,000/- towards permanent alimony and that she would not make any claim for maintenance in future or enhancement of maintenance.

Hon'ble Apex Court held, while dismissing/allowing the appeals:

Delay condoned.

The question that is raised for consideration in this case is whether a compromise entered into by husband and wife under Order XXIII Rule 3 of the Code of Civil Procedure (Code of Civil Procedure), agreeing for a consolidated amount towards permanent alimony, thereby giving up any future claim for maintenance, accepted by the Court in a proceeding Under Section 125 of the Code of Criminal Procedure (Code of Criminal Procedure), would preclude the wife from claiming maintenance in a suit filed Under Section 18 of the Hindu Adoption and Maintenance Act, 1956 (for short "the Act').

After the marriage Petitioner is not maintaining his wife, Respondent filed an application Under Section 125 Code of Criminal Procedure for grant of maintenance before the 1st Additional JMFC at Gulbarga. During the duration of the filed matter pending an application was preferred by the parties under Order XXIII Rule 3 Code of Civil Procedure stating that the parties had arrived at a compromise, by which the Respondent had agreed to receive an amount of Rs. 8,000/- towards permanent alimony and that she would not make any claim for maintenance in future or enhancement of maintenance.

CHAPTER FOURTEEN

CHATURBHUJ VS. SITA BAI, 2007

Hon'ble Judges/Coram:

Dr. Arijit Pasayat and Aftab Alam, JJ.

Relevant Section:

CRIMINAL MATTERS - MATTERS RELATING TO MAINTENANCE UNDER SECTION 125 OF CR.P.C.

No. of pdf pages of the Original Judgment: 4

Equivalent citations:

2007 (Suppl.) ACC 537, 2008(2)BLJ46, IV(2007)CCR408(SC), 2008-1-LW(Crl)615, 2008(1)RCR(Civil)136, 2007(13)SCALE402 MANU/SC/8286/2007

Case Notes:

Code of Criminal Procedure, 1973 - Section 125-Maintenance to wife-Maintenance of Rs. 1,500 per month granted by trial court-Maintained by revisional court and High Court - Whether any interference called for?-Held, "no"-All three courts below analysed evidence-And held that wife was unable to maintain herself-Conclusions essentially factual-And not perverse. (2) Code of Criminal Procedure, 1973 - Section 125-Maintenance to wife-Initial burden placed on wife to show that means of husband sufficient-And that wife was unable to maintain herself-If wife earning some income-To be shown that with amount so earned-She was able to maintain herself.

Facts:

Challenge in this appeal is to the order passed by a learned Single Judge of the Madhya Pradesh High Court, Indore Bench, dismissing the revision petition filed by the appellant in terms of Section 482 of the Code of

Criminal Procedure, 1973 (in short 'Cr.P.C.'). The challenge before the High Court was to the order passed by learned Judicial Magistrate, First Class, Neemuch, M.P. as affirmed by the learned Additional Sessions Judge, Neemuch, M.P. The respondent had filed an application under Section 125 of Cr.P.C. claiming maintenance from the appellant. Undisputedly, the appellant and the respondent had entered into marital knot about four decades back and for more than two decades they were living separately. In the application it was claimed that she was unemployed and unable to maintain herself. Appellant had retired from the post of Assistant Director of Agriculture and was getting about Rs. 8,000/- as pension and a similar amount as house rent. Besides this, he was lending money to people on interest. The appellant claimed Rs. 10,000/- as maintenance. The stand of the appellant was that the applicant was living in the house constructed by the present appellant who had purchased 7 bighas of land in Ratlam in the name of the applicant. She let out the house on rent and since 1979 was residing with one of their sons. The applicant sold the agricultural land on 13.3.2003. The sale proceeds were still with the applicant. The appellant was getting pension of about Rs. 5,700/- p.m. and was not getting any house rent regularly. He was getting 2-3 thousand rupees per month. The plea that the appellant had married another lady was denied. It was further submitted that the applicant at the relevant point of time was staying in the house of the appellant and electricity and water dues were being paid by him. The applicant can maintain herself from the money received from the sale of agricultural land and rent. Considering the evidence on record, the trial Court found that the applicant-respondent did not have sufficient means to maintain herself.

Hon'ble Apex Court held, while dismissing/allowing the appeals:

Leave granted.

Revision petition was filed by the present appellant. Challenge was to the direction to pay Rs. 1500/- p.m. by the trial Court. The stand was that the applicant was able to maintain herself from her income was reiterated. The revisional court analysed the evidence and held that the appellant's monthly income was more than Rs. 10,000/- and the amount received as rent by the respondent-claimant was not sufficient to maintain herself. The revision was accordingly dismissed. The matter was further carried before the High Court by filing an application in terms of Section 482 Cr.P.C. The High Court noticed that the conclusions have been arrived at on appreciation of evidence and, therefore, there is no scope for any interference.

CHAPTER FIFTEEN

SHABANA BANO VS. IMRAN KHAN, 2009

Hon'ble Judges/Coram:

B. Sudershan Reddy and Deepak Verma, JJ.

Relevant Section:

CRIMINAL MATTERS - MATTERS RELATING TO MAINTENANCE UNDER SECTION 125 OF CR.P.C.

No. of pdf pages of the Original Judgment: 6

Equivalent citations:

2010(1)ACR187(SC), 2010(85)AIC227, AIR2010SC305, 2010(1)ALD(Cri)599, 2010 (68) ACC 284, 2010(1)ALT(Cri)159, 2010((1))ALT(Cri)159, 2010(2)BLJ51, 2010(1)BomCR752, IV(2009)CCR557(SC), 2010(2)CGLJ225, 2010CriLJ521, 2009(4)Crimes289(SC), 2010(1)CTC121, 2010GLH(1)416, 2010(1)HLR348, 2010(1)JLJ250(SC), 2010(1)MPHT446(SC), 2010(II)MPJR(SC)127, 2009(1)MPLJ376, 2010MPLJ438(SC), 2010(1)N.C.C.454, 2010(I)OLR5, 2010(I)OLR(SC)5, 2010(1)RCR(Criminal)158, RLW2010(1)SC566, 2009(14)SCALE331, (2009)1SCC666, [2009]1SCR190, 2010(1)UC114, 2010(1)UJ186. MANU/SC/1859/2009

Case Notes:

Code of Criminal Procedure, 1973 - Section 125-Muslim Women (Protection of Rights on Divorce) Act, 1986-Sections 3 and 4-Maintenance - Whether Muslim divorced woman entitled to claim maintenance from her husband under Section 125, Cr. P.C. after expiry of period of iddat also?-Held, "yes" as long as she does not remarry-Matter remitted to Family court for disposal on merits. Danial Latifi and another v. Union of India, (2001) 7

SCC 740 (Const. Bench) and Iqbal Bano v. State of U. P. and another, (2007) 6 SCC 785 : 2007 (3) CCSC 1152 : 2007 (3) ACR 2898 (SC), applied.

Code of Criminal Procedure, 1973 - Section 125-Family Courts Act, 1984 - Section 20-Family Court-Jurisdiction-It has exclusive jurisdiction over matters relating to maintenance including proceedings under Section 125, Cr. P.C.

Facts:

According to the appellant, at the time of marriage, necessary household goods to be used by the couple were given. However, despite this, the respondent-husband and his family members treated the appellant with cruelty and continued to demand more dowry. After some time, the appellant became pregnant and was taken to her parents' house by the respondent. The respondent threatened the appellant that in case his demand of dowry is not met by the appellant's parents, then she would not be taken back to her matrimonial home even after delivery. Appellant delivered a child in her parental home. Since even after delivery, respondent did not think it proper to discharge his responsibility by taking her back.

Hon'ble Apex Court held, while dismissing/allowing the appeals:

Leave granted.

Notwithstanding anything contained in the foregoing provisions of this Act or in any other law for the time being in force, where a Magistrate is satisfied that a divorced woman has not re-married and is not able to maintain herself after the iddat period, he may make an order directing such of her relatives as would be entitled to inherit her property on her death according to Muslim law to pay such reasonable and fair maintenance to her as he may determine fit and proper, having regard to the needs of the divorced woman, the standard of life enjoyed by her during her marriage and the means of such relatives and such maintenance shall be payable by such relatives in the proportions in which they would inherit her property and at such periods as he may specify in his order:

Provided that where such divorced woman has children, the Magistrate shall order only such children to pay maintenance to her, and in the event of any such children being unable to pay such maintenance, the Magistrate shall order the parents of such divorced woman to pay maintenance to her:

Provided further that if any of the parents is unable to pay his or her share of the maintenance ordered by the Magistrate on the ground of his or her not having the means to pay the same, the Magistrate may, on proof of such inability being furnished to him, order that the share of such relatives in the maintenance ordered by him be paid by such of the other relatives as may appear to the Magistrate to have the means of paying the same in such proportions as the Magistrate may think fit to order.

The appellant's petition under Section 125 of the Cr.P.C. would be maintainable before the Family Court as long as appellant does not remarry. The amount of maintenance to be awarded under Section 125 of the Cr.P.C. cannot be restricted for the iddat period only.

In the light of the aforesaid discussion, the impugned orders are hereby set aside and quashed. It is held that even if a Muslim woman has been divorced, she would be entitled to claim maintenance from her husband under Section 125 of the Cr.P.C. after the expiry of period of iddat also, as long as she does not remarry.

As a necessary consequence thereof, the matter is remanded to the Family Court at Gwalior for its disposal on merits at an early date, in accordance with law. The respondent shall bear the cost of litigation of the appellant.

Consequently, the appeal stands allowed to the extent indicated above.

CHAPTER SIXTEEN

SHALU OJHA VS. PRASHANT OJHA, 2018

Hon'ble Judges/Coram:

A.K. Sikri and Ashok Bhushan, JJ.

Relevant Section:

CRIMINAL MATTERS - MATTERS RELATING TO HARASSMENT, CRUELTY TO WOMAN FOR DOWRY, DOWRY DEATH, EVE-TEASING, DOMESTIC VIOLENCE ETC.

No. of pdf Pages of the Original Judgment: 7

Equivalent Citation:

2018(189)AIC267, AIR2018SC3693, 2018 (2) ALD(Crl.) 771 (SC), 2018 (104) ACC 996, 2018 (3) ALT (Crl.) 1 (A.P.), 2018(3)BLJ171, 2018(3)BomCR(Cri)594, 2018 (3) CCC 400 , III(2018)CCR197(SC), 2018CriLJ4040, 2018(3)Crimes428(SC), II(2018)DMC788SC, 2018(3)ECrN 412, 2018(3)JCC1957, 2018(3)JKJ93[SC], 2018(3)N.C.C.131, 2018(3)RCR(Criminal)1004, 2019(1)RLW173(SC), 2018(9)SCALE127, (2018)8SCC452, 2018(2)UC1185 MANU/SC/0763/2018

Case Note:

Family - Maintenance - Reduction of - Section 12 of Protection of Women from Domestic Violence Act, 2005 - Petitioner had filed application claiming maintenance under provisions of Section 12 of Act, which was allowed by Family Court - ASJ decided appeal of Respondent reducing maintenance as fixed by Family Court - Petitioner had filed petition before High Court same was still pending - Notwithstanding, Petitioner had chosen to file instant special leave petition challenging order passed by ASJ - Hence, present appeal - Whether impugned order of reduction of maintenance warrant any interference.

Facts:

The Petitioner had filed an application claiming maintenance under the provisions of Section 12 of the DV Act. The Family Court allowed application filed under Section 12 of the Act. The ASJ decided the appeal of the Respondent reducing the maintenance, as fixed by the Family Court. This order was challenged by the Appellant by filing a petition before High Court which was still pending. Notwithstanding, the Petitioner had chosen to file the instant special leave petition challenging the order passed by the ASJ.

Hon'ble Apex Court held, while dismissing/allowing the appeals:

Held, while disposing of the petition:

(i) The present proceedings arise out of the petition which was filed by the Petitioner under Section 12 of the DV Act. The trial court had arrived at a figure of maintenance on the basis of affidavits filed by both the parties along with their respective documents. Same exercise was undertaken by the ASJ in the impugned order while adjudging the correctness of the order passed by the trial court and, in the process, reducing the maintenance. This obviously happened as the proceedings under the DV Act were of summary nature.

(ii) Thus, the appropriate course of action would be to allow the Petitioner to file an application for maintenance under the Hindu Adoptions and Maintenance Act, 1956 or under Section 125 of the Code of Criminal Procedure, 1973 so that in these proceedings, both the parties lead their documentary and oral evidence and on the basis of such material, appropriate view was taken by the said Court.

CHAPTER SEVENTEEN

Vimalben Ajitbhai Patel and Ors. Vs. Vatslabeen Ashokbhai Patel and Ors., 2008

Hon'ble Judges/Coram:

S.B. Sinha and V.S. Sirpurkar, JJ.

Relevant Section:

HINDU ADOPTIONS AND MAINTENANCE ACT, 1956—SECTION 3(b), 4, 18, 19 AND 28--MAINTENANCE OF WIFE

No. of pdf Pages of the Original Judgment: 12

Equivalent Citation:

AIR2008SC2675, 2008(5)ALD99(SC), 2008 (71) ALR 482, 2009(2)ALT22(SC), 2008 (2) AWC 1636 (SC), 2008(5)BomCR441, CLT(2008)Supp.Crl.986, 2008(2)Crimes45(SC), (2009)1GLR200(SC), [2008(3)JCR14(SC)], JT2008(3)SC530, 2008(2)RCR(Criminal)699, RLW2008(4)SC3440, 2008(4)SCALE601, (2008)4SCC649, 2008(8)UC841 MANU/SC/7334/2008

Case Note:

Hindu Adoptions and Maintenance Act, 1956--Section 3(b), 4, 18, 19 and 28--Maintenance of wife--Personal obligations of mother in law--Held--Personal obligations are on husband only--Property of mother in law can neither be subject matter of attachment nor during life time of husband his personal liability to maintain his wife can be directed to be enforced against such property--Decree if any must be executed against her husband or his properties but not of her mother in law.

Facts:

Personal obligations of mother in law--Held--Personal obligations are on husband only--Property of mother in law can neither be subject matter of attachment nor during life time of husband his personal liability to maintain his wife can be directed to be enforced against such property--Decree if any must be executed against her husband or his properties but not of her mother in law.

Ratio Decidendi : Property in the name of the mother-in-law can neither be a subject matter of attachment nor during the life time of the husband.

Hon'ble Apex Court held, while dismissing/allowing the appeals:

Leave granted in both the matters.

These two appeals being inter related were taken up together for hearing and are being disposed of by the common judgment.

According to Section 20 of the Hindu Adoptions and Maintenance Act, 1956, a Hindu is under a legal obligation to maintain his wife, minor sons, unmarried daughters and aged or infirm parents. The obligation to maintain them is personal, legal and absolute in character and arises from the very existence of the relationship between the parties. But the question before us is whether a stepmother can claim maintenance from the stepson under Section 125 of the Code. In other words, whether Section 125 of the Code includes within its fold the stepmother also as one of the persons to claim maintenance from her stepson.

This provision clearly indicates that if the widowed daughter-in-law is a destitute and has no earnings of her own or other property and if she has nothing to fall back upon for maintenance on the estate of her husband or father or mother or from the estate of her son or daughter, if any, then she can fall back upon the estate of her father-in-law. This provision also indicates that in case of a widowed daughter-in-law of the family if she has no income of her own or no estate of her husband to fall back upon for maintenance, then she can legitimately claim maintenance from her father or mother. On the facts of the present case, therefore, it has to be held that Appellant 1, who was a destitute widowed daughter of the testator and who was staying with him and was being maintained by him in his lifetime, had nothing to fall back upon so far as her deceased husband's estate was concerned and she had no estate of her own. Consequently, as per Section

19(1)(a) she could claim maintenance from the estate of her father even during her father's lifetime. This was a pre-existing right of the widowed daughter qua testator's estate in his own lifetime and this right which was tried to be crystallised in the Will in her favour after his demise fell squarely within the provisions of Section 22(2) of the Maintenance Act.

The High Court committed a manifest illegality in directing cancellation of bail in so far as it failed to take into consideration that the factors relevant for setting aside an order granting bail and directing cancellation of bail arc wholly distinct and different. An application for cancellation of bail must be premised on the factors envisaged under Sub-section (2) of Section 439 of the Code of Criminal procedure. The learned Metropolitan Magistrate in passing the order dated 27th June, 2006 while granting bail took into consideration all the relevant factors. He imposed a fine on them. Even the passports had been surrendered. Application for cancellation of bail was filed on a mis-statement that the passports had not been surrendered. Various contentions, as noticed hereinbefore, in regard to purported suffering of the wife appears to have been taken into consideration which were wholly irrelevant. We have noticed hereinbefore that such contentions have also been raised before us not on the basis that there exists and legal principle behind the same but as an argument of desperation.

A bare perusal of the decision of this Court demonstrates that the ratio laid therein runs counter to the submissions of the learned Counsel.

The appeals are allowed with the aforesaid directions.

I.A. for direction Dismissed.

CHAPTER EIGHTEEN

SHOME NIKHIL DANANI VS. TANYA BANON DANANI, 2019

Hon'ble Judges/Coram:

Dr. D.Y. Chandrachud and Indira Banerjee, JJ.

Relevant Section:

CRIMINAL MATTERS - MATTERS RELATING TO HARASSMENT, CRUELTY TO WOMAN FOR DOWRY, DOWRY DEATH, EVE-TEASING, DOMESTIC VIOLENCE ETC.

No. of pdf Pages of Original Judgment: 2

Equivalent Citation:

2019(3)HLR341, 2019(3)RLW2124(SC) MANU/SC/1192/2019

Case Notes:

Protection of Women from Domestic Violence Act, 2005, Section 18 to 23 read with Code of Criminal Procedure, 1973, Section 125 - 'Maintenance' order passed Under Section 125 Code of Criminal Procedure--Whether it is bar to seeking appropriate reliefs under the Protection of Women from Domestic Violence Act?--Held--Mere passing of a maintenance order Under Section 125 Code of Criminal Procedure does not bar an 'aggrieved person' from seeking appropriate reliefs under the Act of 2005.

SLP dismissed.

Facts:

The High Court of Delhi was justified in coming to the conclusion that the mere passing of an order Under Section 125 of the Code of Criminal Procedure 1973 did not preclude the Respondent from seeking appropriate reliefs under the Protection of Women from Domestic Violence Act 2005.

Hon'ble Apex Court held, while dismissing/allowing the appeals:

Having heard Ms Geeta Luthra, learned senior Counsel for the Petitioner and Ms Vibha Datta Makhija, learned senior Counsel for the Respondent, we are of the view that the High Court of Delhi was justified in coming to the conclusion that the mere passing of an order Under Section 125 of the Code of Criminal Procedure 1973 did not preclude the Respondent from seeking appropriate reliefs under the Protection of Women from Domestic Violence Act 2005. Hence, we decline to entertain the special leave petition Under Article 136 of the Constitution. The special leave petition is accordingly dismissed.

However, we only clarify that any observations made by the High Court on the merits of the claim of the Respondent Under Section 23 shall not come in the way of the appropriate court taking a view on the merits of the matter.

CHAPTER NINETEEN

SHAIL VS. MANOJ KUMAR AND ORS., 2004

Hon'ble Judges/Coram:

R.C. Lahoti, Ashok Bhan and Arun Kumar, JJ

Relevant Sections:

CONTEMPT OF COURT MATTERS - CRIMINAL CONTEMPT MATTERS

No. of pdf Pages of the Original Judgment: 2

Equivalent Citation:

2005(2)ACR1230(SC), 2004(18)AIC369, 2004(2)ALD(Cri)8, 2005 (Suppl.) ACC 362, 2004 (55) ALR 719, 2004(4)ALT11(SC), 2004(2)BLJR1112, 2004(106(4))BOMLR106, II(2004)CCR183(SC), 2004(2)HLR99, JT2004(4)SC391, 2004(3)MhLj503, 2004(3)MhLJ503(SC), 2004MPLJ336(SC), 2004(3)PLJR131, 2005(1)RCR(Criminal)384, 2004(4)SCALE199, (2004)4SCC785, [2004]3SCR649 MANU/SC/0311/2004

Case Notes:

Code of Criminal Procedure, 1973 - Section 125--Maintenance to wife--Application by wife--Delay in disposal--Applicant approaching High Court under Article 227 of Constitution of India--If convinced that deserted woman is on verge of destitution--High Court itself has jurisdiction to direct suitable amount of maintenance being awarded--And to secure compliance with its directions--Petitioner directed to appear before High Court.

Facts:

The facts of this case disclose an uncommon story, the petitioner was victim of an offence under Section 376 and 328 of Indian Penal Code at the hands of the respondent Manoj Kumar. To save himself from the peril of conviction, the respondent agreed to enter into a marriage with the petitioner and the petitioner too agreed to do so. The dream of happy married life soon turned out to be a nightmare as the petitioner was deserted by the respondent. On these averments the petitioner filed an application under Section 125 Cr.P.C. seeking maintenance before the Principal Judge, Family Court, Khanpur Nagar, The delay in disposal of the application persuaded the petitioner to knock the doors of the High Court. The High Court showed indulgence to the petitioner by directing the Family Court to expeditiously conclude the proceedings. As no substantial relief was forthcoming, the petitioner this time invoked the contempt jurisdiction of the High Court complaining of non-compliance with the orders of the High Court by the Presiding Judge, Family Court. By order dated 29.10.2003, the learned Judge of the High Court has expressed his anguish having found a prima facie case of non-compliance with the orders of the High Court having been made out. The High Court has directed summoning of the Presiding Judge of the Family Court to appear before the High Court in-person for the purpose of framing charges for willfully disobeying the orders of the High Court. The petitioner seeks leave to file appeal against the order of the High Court, Her grievance is that the initiation of the proceedings in contempt is alright but then she has been left still high and dry as no relief has been allowed to her. Appearing in-person, she submits that the High Court ought to have directed award of maintenance to her and ought to have seen to some relief being granted to her so as to save her from destitution.

Hon'ble Apex Court held, while dismissing/allowing the appeals:

The delay in disposal of the application persuaded the petitioner to knock the doors of the High Court. The High Court showed indulgence to the petitioner by directing the Family Court to expeditiously conclude the proceedings. As no substantial relief was forthcoming, the petitioner this time invoked the contempt jurisdiction of the High Court complaining of non-compliance with the orders of the High Court by the Presiding Judge, Family Court. By order dated 29.10.2003, the learned Judge of the High Court has expressed his anguish having found a prima facie case of non-compliance with the orders of the High Court having been made out. The High Court has directed summoning of the Presiding Judge of the Family Court to appear before the High Court in-person for the purpose of framing charges for willfully disobeying the orders of the High Court. The petitioner seeks leave to file appeal against the order of the High Court, Her grievance is that the initiation of the proceedings in contempt is alright but then she has been left still high and dry as no relief has been allowed to her. Appearing in-person, she submits that the High Court ought to have directed award of maintenance to her and ought to have seen to some relief being granted to her so as to save her from destitution.

There is nothing in the impugned order by which the petitioner may feel aggrieved. Let the petitioner appear before the High Court on the next date of hearing and seek appropriate interim and urgent relief from the High Court which if deserving, we have no reason to assume why the High Court shall not grant to the petitioner.

The special leave petition be treated as disposed of.

CHAPTER TWENTY

Jaiminiben Hirenbhai Vyas Vs. Hirenbhai Rameshchandra Vyas, 2014

Hon'ble Jugdes/Coram:

Jasti Chelameswar and S.A. Bobde, JJ.

Relevant Sections:

CRIMINAL MATTERS - MATTERS RELATING TO MAINTENANCE UNDER SECTION 125 OF CR.P.C.

No. of pdf Pages of Original Judgments: 4

Equivalent Citation:

2014(3)ACR3346, 2015(146)AIC223, AIR2015SC300, 2015(1)AJR148, 2015(2) AKR 158, 2015 (1) ALD(Crl.) 627 (SC), 2015 (90) ACC 791, 2015ALLMR(Cri)376(SC), 2015 (1) ALT (Crl.) 398 (SC), 2015(1)BLJ13, IV(2014)CCR517(SC), 2015CriLJ608, 2014(6)CTC460, III(2014)DMC737SC, (2015)2GLR953(SC), 2015(1)HLR583, 2015(1)J.L.J.R.29, 2015(1)JCC355, 2015-1-LW(Crl)631, 2015(2)N.C.C.15, 2015(I)OLR245, 2015(1)PLJR201, 2015(1)RCR(Civil)40, 2015(1)RCR(Criminal)84, 2015(2)RLW1162(SC), 2014(13)SCALE104, (2015)2SCC385, 2015 (1) SCJ 216, 2015(1)UC54, 2015 (1) WLN 176 (SC) MANU/SC/1046/2014

Case Notes:

Family - Grant of maintenance - Date of payment - Determination thereof - Section 125 of Criminal Procedure Code, 1973 and Section 24 of Hindu Marriage Act, 1955 - High Court reversed Family Court's order and granted maintenance to Appellant-Wife - However, maintenance was granted from date of order - Hence, present appeal - Whether High Court ought to have granted maintenance from date of application for maintenance instead of date of order - Held, maintenance could be awarded from date of order, or, if so ordered, from date of application for maintenance, as case might be - For awarding maintenance from date of application, express order was necessary - High Court had not given any reason for not granting maintenance from date of application - Circumstances eminently justified grant of maintenance with effect from date of application in view of finding that Appellant had worked before marriage and had not done so during her marriage - There was no evidence of her income during period parties lived as man and wife - Respondent had been directed to pay maintenance from date of application for maintenance - Impugned order reversed - Appeal allowed.

Facts:

On the Appellant's application for maintenance made for herself and her children, the Family Court granted maintenance in the sum of Rs. 5,000/- only to her daughter Under Section 125 Code of Criminal Procedure The son was living with the father who was maintaining him and was therefore not granted maintenance. The main ground for denying maintenance to the Appellant was that she was found to have been working before her marriage and the Family Court was of the view that she could earn her living even now after the separation and therefore she was denied maintenance. This view did not find favour with the High Court, which noted that the Appellant had stopped working after her marriage and had given birth to two children. She had been only looking after the family and had therefore stopped working. The High Court thus reversed the Order of the Family Court and granted maintenance in the sum of Rs. 5,000/-. This was however granted from the date of the order.

Hon'ble Apex Court held, while dismissing/allowing the appeals:

Leave granted.

Section 125 of the Code of Criminal Procedure, therefore, impliedly requires the Court to consider making the order for maintenance effective from either of the two dates, having regard to the relevant facts. For good reason, evident from its order, the Court may choose either date. It is neither appropriate nor desirable that a Court simply states that maintenance should be paid from either the date of the order or the date of the application in matters of maintenance. Thus, as per Section 354(6) of the Code of Criminal Procedure, the Court should record reasons in support of the order passed by it, in both eventualities. The purpose of the provision is to prevent vagrancy and destitution in society and the Court must apply its mind to the options having regard to the facts of the particular case.

In the case before us, the High Court has not given any reason for not granting maintenance from the date of the application. We are of the view that the circumstances eminently justified grant of maintenance with effect from the date of the application in view of the finding that the Appellant had worked before marriage and had not done so during her marriage. There was no evidence of her income during the period the parties lived as man and wife. We, therefore reverse the Order of the High Court in this regard and direct that the Respondent shall pay the amount of maintenance found payable from the date of the application for maintenance. As far as maintenance granted Under Section 24 of the H.M. Act by the Courts below is concerned, it shall remain unaltered.

Accordingly, the appeal is allowed.

Videos & Tv Shows On Law & Exim

List of some important videos & TV shows on Law & EXIM by Adv. Jayprakash Somani on his YouTube Channel 'Jayprakash Somani EXIM & Legal'

Legal Videos: Hindi -English

1) SLP in Supreme Court / Special Leave Petitions in the Supreme Court of India

2) Transfer of Civil & Criminal Cases by the Supreme Court of India / Transfer of Matrimonial Cases

3) Appellate Jurisdiction of the Supreme Court of India

4) Jurisdictions of the Supreme Court of India

5) Public Interest Litigation in the Supreme Court of India / PIL in Supreme Court

6) Article 32 Writ Petitions in the Supreme Court of India

7) Bail Matters Top 10 Supreme Court Cases

8) FIR Quashing in High Court & Supreme Court

9) Bail & Anticipatory Bail Matters in Supreme Court

10) Insolvency & Bankruptcy Matters in the Supreme Court

11) Insolvency & Bankruptcy Code 2016 Part 1

12) Insolvency & Bankruptcy Code 2016 Part 2

13) Insolvency & Bankruptcy Code 2016 Part 3

14) Corporate Liquidation Process

15) Supreme Court Rules & Procedures Webinar of 2.5 hour on Zoom

16) RDDBFI Act, 1993 (Introduction)

17) The Indian Contact Act 1872

18) Negotiable Instruments Act (Introduction)

19) How to avoid matrimonial disputes& some more videos

20) SEBI Matters in the Supreme Court

21) Matrimonial Matters: Supreme Court's 20 Case Laws

22) Consumer Matters Supreme Court's 20 Case Laws

23) Service Matters Supreme Court's 20 Case Laws

24) How to Search Lawyer for Your Matter

25) Property Matters Supreme Court's 20 Case Laws

26) Bail Matters: Supreme Court's 20 Case Laws

27) Supreme Court / High Court Vacation Benches

28) 69000 Teacher's Recruitment Matters of UP Government in the Supreme Court

29) Contempt of Court Matters in the Supreme Court

30) Advocate Act's Matters in the Supreme Court

31) Business Law Matters in the Supreme Court

32) Banking Matters in the Supreme Court

33) Labour Law Matters in the Supreme Court

34) Arbitration Matters in the Supreme Court

35) Careers in Law -Zoom Webinar by Adv. Jayprakash Somani

36) Civil Matters in the Supreme Court

37) Consumer Protection Act | Consumer Matters in the Supreme Court

38) Corporate Matters in the Supreme Court

39) Criminal Matters in the Supreme Court

40) Role of Respondent in the Supreme Court of India

41) Motor Vehicle Accident Matters in Supreme Court with case laws

42) Article 131 Original Suits in Supreme Court

43) PIL in Supreme Court/ Public Interest Litigations in the Supreme Court of India'

44) CAB Citizenship Amendment Bill is not Unconstitutional

45) Supreme Court of India Cases & Process – Marathi

46) Legal Services Export / Export of Legal Services

47) Transfer of Matrimonial Cases by the Supreme Court of India

48) Public Interest Litigation PIL

49) The Specific Relief Act (Introduction)

50) Corporate Insolvency Resolution Process CIRP

51) ABMM's Career 5 - Careers in Law

52) Transfer of cases by Supreme Court

53) Writ Petitions in High Court & Supreme Court of India

54) Supreme Court Jurisdictions - Appeals, SLP, Writ Petitions, Transfer, Original, Review, Curative

55) LEGAL INDIA TV Show: Cases Handled in Supreme Court

56) Corporate Liquidation Process

57) Legal Services Export / Export of Legal Services

58) Corporate Laws

59) Election Matters- Supreme Court's 20 Case Laws

60) Companies Act, 2013

62) Competition Act, 2002

63) Banking Matters - Supreme Court's 20 Case Laws

64) Election Matters in the Supreme Court

65) Armed Forces Tribunal Matters in the Supreme Court

66) Compassionate Appointment Service matter

67) Foreign Exchange Management Act FEMA

68) Foreign Trade Policy 2021-26 Proposed

69) Customs Act 1962

70) Narcotic Drugs and Psychotropic Substances Act, 1985 NDPS Act

71) Foreign Trade Development & Regulation Act, 1992

72) How to Search Good Advocate in the Supreme Court of India

73) Sr. Adv Vikas Singh's Interview in Nani Palkhivala Wednesday Law Club

EXIM Videos: Hindi -English

1) Yes, I can do Import Export Business Easily! 36 points excellent video in Hindi

2) Yes, I can do Import Export Business Easily! 36 points excellent video in English

3) Import Export Business – Hindi video

4) Import Export Business - English video

5) Export Import Marathi TV Interview

6) Scope for Commerce Students in International Business- TV Show

7) Scope for Management Student in International Business- TV Show

8) Scope for Engineering Students in International Business – TV Show

9) Women in International Business- TV Show

10) How to do Import Export Business Successfully!'

11) Where one can get full information on Import Export Business?

12) What to do import & export?

13) Import Export Workshop/ Training/Course/ Diploma

14) How to Start Import Export Business & How to grow it. Live Webinar

15) Success Stories & Failure Stories in Import & Export Business

16) For MSME Scope in Export & Import...

17) Exports In Agri. & Food Products – English & some more videos

18) Exports to Dubai, Aabudhabii. e. UAE

19) Jewellery Exports from India

20) How to attend EXIM workshop to become excellent Exporter

21) Import Export Best Training Course – Online & Offline

22) Agri Product Export

23) Scope for Woman in International Business

24) Management Graduates Scope in International Business

25) Pharma Product's Export

26) Best Import Export Course | Practical Training | Aaronica Global Exim

27) Import Export Business for Commerce Graduates

28) How Do I Get Export Orders? Finding International Buyers

29) What Is APEDA In Import Export Business?

30) Which Is The Best Product To Export From India?

31) EXIM Remark by Manoj Kumar Faridabad

32) EXIM Remarks by Mahesh Telangana

33) What Licenses I Need To Start Import/ Export?

34) How Can I Increase My Import Export Business?

35) Which Is Best B2B Website For Import/Export Business?

36) Export Import Management with Global Marketing

37) How to Start Export Import Business | 51 Points Video

38) Scope for Commerce & Other Graduates in International Business

39) BE A SUCCESSFUL EXPORTER FOR OUR NATION - Marathi video

40) Export of Textile , Cotton, Agri., Food, & other products & services

41) Exports from MP, CG, MH, GJ & CA in Fresh Fruits & Vegetables

42) Exports in Agri. & Food Products- Hindi

43) Start your Online/E-Commerce Business

44) How to Start Export Import Business & Grow it

45) Exports in Textile & Other Products

46) Start and grow EXIM business - Live English Webinar

47)'Import Export Business!‘ Why, Who, What & How can one do it easily!!

48) Live: Export of Product & Services During & After Lock Down Period

49) Frauds in Import Export Business

50) Import Export for Business Man

51) Import & Export for Women

51) Import & Export for Graduate & Post - Graduate Students

52) Agriculture Exports from India

53) Digital Marketing Setup - Marathi

54) 2nd Secret of Successful Businessman

55) Digital Marketing Set up

56) Legal Services Export / Export of Legal Services

57) Export & Import with UAE

58) Service Exports / Exports by Service Providers

59) Import Export Workshop/ Training/Course/ Diploma

60) Exports & Imports with USA

61) Selection on Product for Export

62) Top Products Exported from India

63) What to do import & export?

64) ABMM Career 2 - 'Careers in Business & Industries

65) How to do Import Export Business Successfully!'

66) 5 Secrets of Successful Businessman

67) Export from MP, Chhattisgarh & Vidarbha Nagpur

68) EXIM Hindi - Textile & Apparel Export

69) EXIM Hindi - Export Import Practical Training In Delhi, Kolkata, Mumbai and Pune

70) Import Export Business

71) Import Export Business Hindi

72) Import Export Business English video

73) Import Export Business Marathi

74) Women in International Business by Exim Guru Adv. Jayprakash Somani

75) Opportunities in Foreign Trade- Adv. Jayprakash Somani's special interview

76) Textile Exports

77) India's Number in Exports. How to improve it?

78) 11 Benefits of Exim Workshop

79) Export Import Management with Global Marketing- 13 days Training Workshop

80) Cosmetic's Export

82) Export After COVID

83) Spices Exports

84) Handicraft Export

85) 10 Products India Exports to the World

List Of Books

1. Supreme Court of India's Leading Case Laws on 'Insolvency & Bankruptcy Code 2016'

2. Bail Matters – Supreme Court's Latest Leading Case Laws

3. Arbitration Matters- Supreme Court's Latest Leading Case Laws

4. Property Matters - Supreme Court's Latest Leading Casc Laws

5. Matrimonial Matters- Supreme Court's Latest Leading Case Laws

6. Election Matters- Supreme Court's Latest Leading Case Laws

7.SEBI Matters- Supreme Court's Latest Leading Case Laws

8. Banking Matters- Supreme Court's Latest Leading Case Laws

9. Service Matters- Supreme Court's Latest Leading Case Laws

10. Contempt of Court Matters- Supreme Court's Latest Leading Case Laws

11. Consumer Protection Matters- Supreme Court's Latest Leading Case Laws

12. Corporate Law- Supreme Court's Latest Leading Case Laws

13. Supreme Court's AOR Exam- Leading Cases

14. Armed Force Tribunal - Supreme Court's Latest Leading Case Laws

15. Acquittal From 376 - Supreme Court's Latest Leading Case Laws

16. Negotiable instrument – Supreme Court's Latest Leading Case Laws

17. Contract Act- Supreme Court's Latest Leading Case Laws

18. Insider trading- Supreme Court's Latest Leading Case Laws

19. Foreign Exchange and Management Act- Supreme Court's Latest Leading Case Laws

20. Income Tax Act- Supreme Court's Latest Leading Case Laws

21. Company Law- Supreme Court's Latest Leading Case Laws

22. Competition & Monopoly Matters- Supreme Court's Latest Leading Case Laws

23. Compassionate Appointment- Service Matters- Supreme Court's Latest Leading Case Laws

24. Compulsory Retirement- Service Matters- Supreme Court's Latest Leading Case Laws

25. Voluntary Retirement- Service Matters- Supreme Court's Latest Leading Case Laws

26. Removal/Dismissal/Termination from Service- Supreme Court's Latest Leading Case Laws

27. Seniority- Service Matter- Supreme Court's Latest Leading Case Laws

28. Promotion- Service Matter- Supreme Court's Latest Leading Case Laws

29. Equal Pay for Equal Work- Service Matter- Supreme Court's Latest Leading Case Laws

30. Condition of Service- Service Matter- Supreme Court's Latest Leading Case Laws

31. Customs Act- Supreme Court's Leading Case Laws

32. Information Technology Act- Supreme Court's Latest Leading Case Laws

33. SEC. 125 CR. P. C.- Supreme Court's Latest Leading Case Laws

These Books are available online at

1. **Notion Press:** https://notionpress.com/author/jayprakash_somani
2. **Amazon:** https://www.amazon.in/s?k=jayprakash+somani
3. **Flipkart:** https://www.flipkart.com/search?q=Jayprakash%20Somani

Printed by Libri Plureos GmbH in Hamburg,
Germany